One Generation After

Translated from the French
by Lily Edelman and the author

NEW YORK

RANDOM HOUSE

One Generation After

Elie Wiesel

Library of Congress Catalog Card
Number: 79-117699

Manufactured in the United States of America
by The Book Press, Brattleboro, Vermont

2 4 6 8 9 7 5 3
First Printing

One Generation
After

ONE GENERATION
AFTER

TWENTY-FIVE YEARS. A quarter-century.

And we pause, trying to find our bearings, trying to understand: what and how much did these years mean? To some a generation, to others an eternity. A generation perhaps without eternity.

Children condemned never to grow old, old men doomed never to die. A solitude engulfing entire peoples, a guilt tormenting all humanity. A despair that found a face but not a name. A memory cursed, yet refusing to pass on its curse and hate. An attempt to understand, perhaps even to forgive. That is a generation.

Ours.

For the new one it will soon be ancient history. Unrelated to today's conflicts and arguments. Without impact on the aspirations and actions of adolescents eager to live and conquer the future. The past interests them only to the extent that they can reject it. Auschwitz? Never heard of it.

And yet there is logic in history. The future is but a result of conditions past and present. Everything is con-

3

nected, everything has its place. Man makes the transition from the era of holocaust silence to the era of communications with remarkable ease. Once walled in by ghettos, man now takes flight to the moon. If today we live too quickly, it is because yesterday we died too quickly. If today we endow machines with increasingly wide powers, it is because the generation before us so foolishly left its fate and decisions in the hands of man.

Spring 1945: emerging from its nightmare, the world discovers the camps, the death factories. The senseless horror, the debasement: the absolute reign of evil. Victory tastes of ashes.

Yes, it is possible to defile life and creation and feel no remorse. To tend one's garden and water one's flowers but two steps away from barbed wire. To experiment with monstrous mutations and still believe in the soul and immortality. To go on vacation, be enthralled by the beauty of a landscape, make children laugh—and still fulfill regularly, day in and day out, the duties of killer.

There was, then, a technique, a science of murder, complete with specialized laboratories, business meetings and progress charts. Those engaged in its practice did not belong to a gutter society of misfits, nor could they be dismissed as just a collection of rabble. Many held degrees in philosophy, sociology, biology, general medicine, psychiatry and the fine arts. There were lawyers among them. And—unthinkable but true—theologians. And aristocrats.

Astounded, the victors find it difficult to accept the facts: that in the twentieth century, man's armor against himself and others should be so thin and vulnerable. Yes, good and evil coexist without the one influencing the other; the devil himself strives for an ideal: he too sees himself as pure and incorruptible. Inherited values count for nothing. Seeds sown by earlier generations? Lost in the sand, blown away by the wind. Nothing is certain, the present erases triumphs and treasures with hallucinating speed. Civilization? Foam that crests the waves and vanishes. Lack of morality and a perverted taste for bloodshed are unrelated to the individual's social and cultural background. It is possible to be born into the upper or middle class, receive a first-rate education, respect parents and neighbors, visit museums and attend literary gatherings, play a role in public life, and begin one day to massacre men, women and children, without hesitation and without guilt. It is possible to fire your gun at living targets and nonetheless delight in the cadence of a poem, the composition of a painting. One's spiritual legacy provides no screen, ethical concepts offer no protection. One may torture the son before his father's eyes and still consider oneself a man of culture and religion. And dream of a peaceful sunset over the sea.

Had the killers been brutal savages or demented sadists, the shock would have been less. And also the disappointment.

Adolf Eichmann was an ordinary man. He slept well, he ate well. He was an exemplary father, a considerate husband. During the trial in Jerusalem, I could not turn my gaze away from him. I stared at him until my eyes burned. Naïvely, I was looking for the mark on his forehead, believing somehow that he who sows death must perforce dig a grave within himself. I was shaken by his normal appearance and behavior.

The way he spoke and pleaded made everything chillingly clear, disgustingly banal. With cool detachment, he expressed himself in a language devoid of irony or vehemence, monotonously reciting dates, figures and reports. At first he frightened me. It occurred to me that if he were sane, I should choose madness. It was he or I. For me, there could be no common ground with him. We could not inhabit the same universe, nor be governed by the same laws.

Yet he was a man like any other.

A metamorphosis was taking place. On many levels and affecting all of humanity: executioners and victims alike. The first too anxious to become executioners, the latter too ready to assume the role of victims. How long did it take? One night, one week. Or more. A year, perhaps three. Time is a lesser factor than man's ability to discard his inner self. To a victim of the "concentrationary" system, it no longer mattered that he had been intellectual, laborer, angry student or devoted husband. A few beatings, a few screams turned him into a blank, his loss of identity complete. He no longer thought as before, nor did he look men straight in the eyes; his own eyes were no longer the same. Camp law and camp truth transcended all laws and all truth, and the prisoner could not help but submit. When he was hungry, he thought of soup and not of immortality. After a long night's march, he yearned for rest and not for mercy. Was this all there was to man?

People wanted to understand: the executioner's fascination with crime, the victim's with death, and what had paved the way for Auschwitz. Explanations alternated with theories involving everything from politics to mass psychosis; none proved adequate. It was like coming up against a dark wall. Auschwitz eluded man to the end. And beyond. Whence the anguish hovering over the post-war generation. It needed to unravel the mystery; pinpoint the attraction the abyss exerts on man and determine the nature of what pushes him to his downfall. To succeed, one would have had to question many executioners and many of the dead. The first had long since escaped, the latter were still without graves.

So we turned to the victims, the survivors. They were asked to bare themselves, to delve into the innermost recesses of their being, and tell, and tell again, to the point of exhaustion and beyond: to the delirium that follows. How it had been. Had the killers really been so many and so conscientious in their task? And the machinery so efficient? Had it really been a universe with its own gods and priests, its own princes with their laws, its philosophers with their disciples? And you, how did you manage to survive? Had you known the art of survival from before? And how were you able to keep your sanity? And today: how can you sleep, work, go to restaurants and movies, how can you mingle with people and share their meals?

People wanted to know everything, resolve all questions, leave nothing in the dark. What frightened them was the mystery.

The survivors were reticent, their answers vague. The subject: taboo. They remained silent. At first out of reserve; there are wounds and sorrows one prefers to conceal. And out of fear as well. Fear above all. Fear of arousing disbelief, of being told: Your imagination is sick, what you describe could not possibly have happened. Or: You are counting on our pity, you are exploiting your suffering. Worse: they feared being inadequate to the task, betraying a unique experience by burying it in worn-out phrases and images. They were afraid of saying what must not be said, of attempting to communicate with language what eludes language, of falling into the trap of easy half-truths.

Sooner or later, every one of them was tempted to seal his lips and maintain absolute silence. So as to transmit a vision of the holocaust, in the manner of certain mystics, by withdrawing from words. Had all of them remained mute, their accumulated silences would have become unbearable: the impact would have deafened the world.

When they agreed to lift the veil, many obstacles and inhibitions had to be overcome. They reassured themselves: This is but a difficult first step. In any event, we are only messengers. With some luck, other men will benefit from our experience. And learn what the individual is capable of doing under a totalitarian regime, when the line between humanity and inhumanity becomes blurred. And what wars are made of and where they lead. They will discover the link between words and the ashes they cover.

How guileless they were, those surviving tellers of tales. They sought to confer a retroactive meaning upon a trial which had none. They thought: Who knows, if we can make ourselves heard, man will change. His very vision of himself will be altered. Thanks to illustrations provided by us, he will henceforth be able to distinguish between what he may or may not do, what goals to pursue or forgo. He could then forge for himself a reality made of desire rather than necessity, a freedom commensurate with his creative impulse rather than with his destructive instinct.

Twenty-five years later, after the reckoning, one feels discouragement and shame. The balance sheet is disheartening. There are even farcical aspects to the situation. In Germany, where Nazism is on the rise again, one finds former killers hiding beneath the respectability of judges, attorneys, businessmen, patrons of the arts, and even clergy. A French politician—and member of Parliament—publicly accuses the Jews of peddling their suffering. Robbed of their property and rights, the Jews in Arab countries live in constant fear. They are slandered in the Soviet Union, persecuted in Poland. And, fact without precedent, anti-Semitism has finally reached China.

Which raises the question for the survivors: Was it not a mistake to testify, and by that very act, affirm their faith in man and word?

I know of at least one who often feels like answering yes.

If society has changed so little, if so many strategists are preparing the explosion of the planet and so many people willingly submit, if so many men still live under oppression and so many others in indifference, only one conclusion is possible: namely, that the failure of the black years has begotten yet another failure. Nothing has been learned; Auschwitz has not even served as warning. For more detailed information, consult your daily newspaper.

If the witness happens to be a storyteller, he will be left with a sense of impotence and guilt. He was wrong to have forced himself upon others, to have badgered a world wishing to take no notice. He was wrong to have thrown open the doors of the sanctuary in flames; people did not look. Worse: many looked and did not see.

Thus, writing itself is called into question. To set oneself the task of bringing back to life the hallucinatory reality of a single human being, in a single camp, borders on sacrilege. The truer the tale, the more factitious it appears. The secret must remain inviolate. Once revealed, it becomes myth, and can only be tarnished, diminished. In the end, words lose their innocence, their power to cast a spell. The truth will never be written. Like the Talmud, it will be transmitted from mouth to ear, from eye to eye. By its uniqueness, the holocaust defies literature. We think we are describing an event, we transmit only its reflection. No one has the right to speak for the dead, no one has the power to make them speak. No image is sufficiently demented, no cry sufficiently blasphemous to illuminate the plight of a single victim, resigned or rebellious, walking silently toward death, beyond anger, beyond regret. With pity perhaps.

Therein lies the dilemma of the storyteller who sees himself essentially as a witness, the drama of the messenger unable to deliver his message: how is one to speak of it, how is one not to speak of it? Certainly there can be no other theme for him: all situations, all conflicts, all obsessions will, by comparison, seem pallid and futile. And yet, how is one to approach this universe of darkness without turning into a peddler of night and agony? Without becoming other?

About Yonathan ben Uziel, the Talmud tells us that he studied Torah with such fervor that flames encircled him —the flames of Sinai—blinding and scorching the birds who flew too close, wanting to see or be warmed. This is true also for the writer grappling with the theme of the holocaust; he will inevitably burn his fingers, and sometimes more.

Still, the story had to be told. In spite of all risks, all possible misunderstandings. It needed to be told for the sake of our children. So they will know where they come from, and what their heritage is. The past carried away by clouds needed to be brought back, and so did the clouds. We needed to face the dead, again and again, in order to appease them, perhaps even to seek among them, beyond all contradiction and absurdity, a symbol, a beginning of promise.

But from here on, there will be a change. Like it or not, a quarter of a century marks a turning point, a line of demarcation. From now on, one will speak differently about the holocaust. Or not at all. At least not for a long time. Other exploits, other explorations even now compete for our attention. The era of the moon opens at the very moment that, reluctantly, the age of Auschwitz comes to a close.

Still, though we already know the dark secret face of our satellite, we will never fully know the other face of Auschwitz. The concentration-camp man will try to seal his memory, the witness promises never again to call him to the stand. The inventory is closed. The ghosts will have to accept the inevitable. Soon there will be no one left to speak of them, no one left to listen.

JOURNEY'S
BEGINNING

A MAN'S LAST VISION of what was his beginning is like no other, for like that beginning, it becomes part of him, irrevocably and unalterably. God Himself cannot change man's past, though man can alter his vision of God. Both are bound by one beginning.

Will I ever forget mine? I look at it and know that it is for the last time. I shall never recapture that look in my eyes. And I shall carry it away like a tune never to be sung again, a secret never to be shared. For the last time I remember.

Twenty-five years separate the witness from the object of his testimony: his native town. Twenty-five years of wandering in a disjointed, often hostile, always irreducible world—searching, questioning, disturbing others and being disturbed himself. And all that time I was looking for something without knowing what it was. Now I know. A small Jewish town, surrounded by mountains. A little town I wanted to enter one last time and leave there all I possess: my memory.

That town. I see it still, I see it everywhere. I see it with such clarity that I often mock and admonish myself: con-

tinue and you'll go mad; the town no longer exists, it never
did. But I can't help it, I see nothing else. Its *tzaddikim*
and troubadours, its sages and their noisy children, its
poverty-striken visionaries and almost equally poor merchants: I see them on the main square, drenched in sweat,
rushing to the market, to school, to religious services, to
the ritual baths, to the cemetery. I even see the cemetery,
though I set foot there only once.

Neighbors, acquaintances, friends: at times their presence
becomes so real that I want to stop one of them, anyone,
and entrust him with a message: Go and tell all those people, your companions and mine, tell them they're taking
the wrong road, they're turning away from their future;
tell them that danger lies in wait, that mankind is at their
heels, hungry for their blood and their death.

But I keep quiet. I am afraid lest that person reply: I
don't believe you, I don't know you. Lest he shrug his
shoulders and continue on the road straight to his tomb
up there, his tomb veiled in incandescent clouds. I want
to shout, to scream, only I am afraid of waking him. It is
dangerous to wake the dead, especially if their memory is
better than yours; it is dangerous to be seen by them,
especially if they have robbed you of your town and childhood, the beginning you are remembering for the last time.

Sighet. A Rumanian, Hungarian, Austrian province.
Occupied by the Turks, the Russians, the Germans, coveted
by all the tribes in that part of the world. Despite the
diversity of tongues spoken, despite the variety of regimes
succeeding one another, it was a typically Jewish town,
such as could be found by the hundreds between the

Dnieper and the Carpathians. Thanks to its dominantly Jewish population, it cleansed itself for Yom Kippur, fasted and lamented the destruction of the Temple on Tishah b'Av, and celebrated Simchat Torah by getting drunk.

You went out into the street on Saturday and felt Shabbat in the air. Stores were closed, business centers at a standstill, municipal offices deserted. For the Jews as well as their Christian neighbors, it was a day of total rest. The old men gathered in synagogues and houses of study to listen to itinerant preachers, the young went strolling in the park, through the woods, along the riverbank. Your concerns, anxieties and troubles could wait: Shabbat was your refuge.

The day before, on Friday afternoon, you could already sense the approaching Shabbat. To welcome it, the men plunged into the ritual baths. The women cleaned house, scrubbed floors, bustled about in the kitchen and prepared their prettiest dresses. Coming home from school, the boys recited the Song of Songs. Then, at the very same moment, the same chant went up in every house: *Shalom aleikhem malakhei hashalom*—Be blessed, O messengers full of blessings, enter and depart in peace, O angels of peace . . .

Everyone, rabbi or illiterate, prosperous storekeeper or porter, employer or employee, everyone addressed the angels of Shabbat with the same words, expressing the same gratitude.

"The angels, who are they?" I once asked my grandfather, whose Wizsnitzer melodies overwhelmed me, so violent and tender was the joy they expressed.

By way of response, he leaned toward me and whispered into my ear a secret which has remained with me to this day: "The angels, my child, the angels are all of us sitting around this table—and other tables like it—covered with a white cloth and transformed into an altar. You, I, all our guests. Therein lies the force and grandeur of Shabbat: it makes it possible for man to fulfill himself by renewing his bonds with his beginning."

And then I heard heavenly wings fluttering above my head—yes, I did hear them, I swear. But since I left you, Grandfather, since I stopped singing your melodies, I have not seen the angels any more, that too I swear. In truth, Grandfather, I think they stayed behind, in our forgotten little town buried in the mountains, invisible like you and me, like all of us.

My grandfather lived in a small village: Bichkev, or Bocsko in Hungarian. There Dodye Feig led the peaceful existence of a farmer. I loved his stories, his songs. And his silences too.

An indefatigable worker, he did everything himself. He fed his cows, tilled his land, and climbed the trees to pick plums, apples and apricots. Every day he waited in the twilight for darkness to fall before lighting the oil lamp. Sitting on his porch, he allowed night and stillness to envelop him.

In the beginning I showed my surprise: "But, Grandfather, I can't see a thing!"

His answers came in a whisper: "You are still young. Later you'll speak otherwise. For the moment, look and be quiet."

I used to visit him during vacations. He himself came to Sighet only for the High Holidays. To attend services across the street from our house, where the Borsher Rebbe attracted hundreds of followers from neighboring villages. I still remember the hours I remained standing behind the Rebbe. I did my best to hitch my prayers to his and thus to pierce the walls of the celestial sanctuary.

One day I saw the Rebbe beat his breast and implore God's forgiveness for his sins. Troubled, I questioned my grandfather: "How is that possible? A Rebbe transgressing the laws of Torah?"

On that occasion my grandfather revealed yet another secret to me: "A person can be innocent and still believe himself guilty."

The following year I wept like the Rebbe, even more than he. Like him I confessed multitudes of sins and crimes, I beat my breast with even greater anguish than he, and finally attracted my grandfather's attention and displeasure.

He ordered me to moderate my fervor: "Who do you think you are? You must not copy the Rebbe's gestures, you are not to imitate him again. You can follow and obey him, but that's all. Don't try to assume his role; one does not reach for the royal scepter with impunity. Even if the king appears to be absent."

Our town boasted other spiritual leaders of great and not so great fame and erudition. Each had his sanctuary, his disciples, his counselors, his benefactors, his happy or unhappy followers—all pleading with God to come to the rescue of men already marked and singled out by destiny. Yet God refused to lend His ear. Consequently Grandfather, I should feel less guilty. But no, on the contrary, my list of avowed sins keeps growing longer and longer, and I am waiting for someone to tell me why.

However, to avoid any possible misunderstanding, let it be stated at once that the Jews of Sighet were not all saints. Many did not spend their time studying sacred texts or reciting psalms. The merchants had their share of faults and weaknesses; they were neither more honest nor more conniving than elsewhere. The rich displayed their wealth while the poor tried to hide their misery. The tailors and shoemakers, the woodcutters and coachmen, confronted daily with despair, did not pretend to be poets in disguise: fraught with malediction, their poverty lacked poetry. Though God's associates and victims, many were not kind or gentle and could not rise above their frustrations and bitterness. They quarreled, they insulted one another and gossiped. Yes, like everywhere else, we had our envious and our liars, misers and thieves, even some perjurers and renegades. Only now, as I look back, do I realize how harmless their vices were. They asked so little of life and society: a bed to sleep on, a book to dream over, a *melamed* to instruct their children, and a sign of consolation, any sign—an assurance that no suffering is in vain. And in return, they were always ready to contribute to the schools, the sick, the poor, the orphans, the unmarried girls, the aged and homeless, the failures and the wanderers. Concerned and generous, they could always be counted on. Whenever any community's honor or survival was threatened, they rose in solidarity to save it.

I remember: a red-faced fellow, deeply offended because he had been refused the privilege of helping a certain cause. He was the town informer, and no one spoke to him. In vain did he protest that his was a trade like any other, that he was not all that dangerous, since everyone knew him; he remained on the fringes of the community. He attended services but was never called to the Torah. In time, he was forced to change towns and eventually trades.

We had our non-believers, naturally, and they too are unforgettable. The most famous was a man over a hundred years old who hated his neighbors, the Hasidim, because their frequent and noisy celebrations disturbed him. He would say: "Since they cannot make themselves heard except by shouting, their heaven must be far away, and that's a pity, especially for me, who live so near."

In his younger days he never went out without his dog. One day, on the street, he met the rabbi accompanied by his servant.

"You're not a rabbi like me, but like me you need a companion to serve you," the rabbi laughingly called out.

"True," replied the non-believer, petting his dog, "except that in my case I am the servant."

This story did not end there. Instead of getting angry, the rabbi put his hand on the non-believer's shoulder and said: "You don't like me, but you love your dog, which means that you do have feelings; in the end that's what counts."

Years later the same man slapped his son for having the impertinence to criticize the rabbi. I never knew the rabbi but I remember his defender.

I remember, I remember.

A madman named Moshe. He was mad only during the summer months, regaining his sanity before the High Holidays. Then he conducted services in a barn with a leaky roof, in a forsaken village which could afford neither rabbi nor cantor. After the holidays he taught the *aleph-bet* to small children whose parents could not pay a regular tutor.

I shall never forget him. Broad-shouldered, heavy-set, and always starving, he had a red bushy beard, and frequently bleeding swollen lips. I can still feel the bite of his fierce, frightened eyes, which, unseen but seeing, lurked behind the two narrow slits carved in his untidy face.

The schoolchildren, cruel and lazy, often persecuted Moshe. He let them. Sometimes he sought refuge in our house. To forget his pain, he would drink and sing. As I listened to him, I felt myself turning into someone else. He frightened and fascinated me; I knew that he moved in a universe all his own. Occasionally I tried to make him speak and describe what he was seeing, what was tormenting him. He preferred to sing.

When I became interested in psychiatry years later, I suspected it was because of Moshe. A friend asked what I was seeking in the world of the insane. I answered: They are alone, and they sing—their silence itself sings. Besides, they see things we do not see.

A second Moshe: the beadle. Weak and shy, he had eyes like a beaten dog, the face and helpless body of a sick child. He accepted defeat in advance, resigned to man's meanness and cruelty.

Stateless, he was among the first "undesirable aliens" to be affected by the expulsion law. When was that? In 1942, I think. How many were deported at that time? A hundred, a thousand. Perhaps more, surely more. I remember: the entire community—men, women and children—accompanied them to the station, bringing along sacks stuffed with food. Then the train pulled away. Destination unknown.

Few came back. One who did was Moshe the Beadle. He was unrecognizable; gone were his gentleness, his shyness. Impatient, irascible, he now wore the mysterious face of a messenger pursued by those whose message he carried. He who used to stutter whenever he had to say a single word, suddenly began to speak. He talked and talked, without pity for either his listeners or himself. He had discovered a new vocation as public speaker and agitator.

He went from one synagogue to the next, from house to house, from store to store, from factory to factory, he spoke to passers-by in the street, farmers in the marketplace. He told and told again tales so heinous as to make your skin crawl. Accounts of his journey somewhere in Galicia, his escape, his experience of death. And his family? Left behind. And his children? Left behind. And his friends? Left behind, over there, at the bottom of a mass grave. Shot, all of them. In broad daylight. He too had been shot, falling only a fraction of a second before it would have been too late. Protected by those who followed, he alone survived. Why? So that he could come back to his town and tell the tale. And that is why he never stopped talking. But his audiences, weary and naïve, would not, could not believe. People said: Poor beadle, he has lost his mind. Finally he understood, and fell silent. Only his burning eyes revealed the impotent rage inside him. His muteness bordered on madness. But he maintained it until two years later, a few days before the last Shavuot, when the fate of our ghetto was already sealed. Then he burst into our house and informed my father of his decision to run away. He left singing: "There is nothing, nothing left for me to do here, I am going, going, going back to Galicia. With a little luck, I'll get there before the holidays, before the burial . . ."

And Leizer—have I told you about him? He had a last name, but it escapes me. I'm not even sure about his nickname. Leizer the Fat, or Leizer the Black—or was it Leizer the Giggler? For he was fat and dirty and used to laugh day and night, endlessly and—above all—without reason. But who ever needed a reason to laugh at the world?

His face was round and scarred, but his eyes twinkled. As he walked, his cumbersome body swayed and his enormous arms dangled back and forth. He slept in the *hekdesh*, the community asylum, and lived by charity. Strange, he never went inside a home, but waited in the courtyard or near the porch, until someone brought him a piece of bread soaked in oil, some boiled potatoes, a glass of fresh milk or a few pennies.

He enjoyed playing with the children as they came home from school. He encouraged them to throw rocks at him and fight. The more they mocked him, the happier he was.

On the other hand, the anti-Semitic ruffians refrained from scuffling with him. He was the only Jew who dared walk the streets on Christmas night. Sheer ignorance or desire to provoke? The fact is, he was never molested. And so I came to see in him a reincarnation of the Golem, that clay creature endowed with strength but not intelligence, invented centuries ago by legend to protect the Jews of Prague. Like them, we were intelligent but weak; we too needed a protector.

Stretched out before the stove just inside the Talmud Torah, Leizer seemed, all through the long winter months, to be awaiting a call. At the approach of Passover, his laughter became nervous and abrupt. I thought I understood why: like the first Golem, the one of Prague, he had to be alert and on the lookout so as to ward off our enemies, who for centuries have hated and persecuted us, particularly during our holidays.

The last time I remember seeing him was the day the ghetto was liquidated. He was in the first convoy. That day he seemed gloomy and angry: someone was preventing him from fulfilling his mission, from confronting the killers head-on and trampling down the bearers of hate and death. He was breathing heavily, like a wounded animal.

I should have noticed that he had stopped laughing. And recognized it as a warning.

Another tale of another beggar, the last. Don't worry: this one concerns the adventures of a prince. For there was one in our town. You'll see. To each and everyone his prince. One prince is driven into hell, another is lifted on to a royal white stallion. The third flies away on the wings of legend. As for mine, he wore no crown, he promised neither moon nor stars, he exacted neither obedience nor honors: he sought nothing. Was he a symbol? If so, no one ever was privileged to find its meaning. Did he possess hidden marvels and treasures? No one ever was privileged to see them.

My prince distinguished himself by neither splendor nor elegance. He was old and his clothes were in tatters. His face was his: he had nothing else.

He was poor, the poorest beggar in our community. Like the others, he slept near the stove in the synagogue. Each morning when I arrived for services, I found him sitting on the last bench, lost in dreams, his eyes reflecting nameless sorrow.

Taciturn and aloof, he rarely solicited alms, at least not by word. There he stood before you, watching you out of the corner of his eyes. Heeded or not, he smiled, stammered a word of thanks and went on his way. Something in his behavior, his awkward gestures, evoked affection more than charity, respect rather than compassion.

We called him Shmukler. Was that his last name or his first? I don't know. Like everyone else, I did know that he had come from far away. He had arrived during World War I, wearing an officer's uniform. Had he been victor or loser? Warden or prisoner? Opinions were divided and he himself refused to clarify the matter. He would listen absent-mindedly, not offering any comments.

Why had he decided to settle in our small town? Why did he not go home—and where was home? The mystery surrounding him gave rise to various theories. He was a business tycoon from Berlin, a celebrated artist from Vienna. His fiancée, in Budapest, was rich and famous for her beauty. Furthermore, she sang at the opera. She was younger than he. No, older than his mother. A drug addict at that. No, he was the one, not she. Was he at least Jewish? He did not understand Yiddish, which in our region was enough to make him suspect. One morning I surprised him in the synagogue, wearing phylacteries on his forehead and left arm: he looked like a different man. Some thought him a penitent, others were convinced he was a convert, an adventurer, a saint, a Lamed Vav, a poet, an escaped criminal: he might have been any of those.

As the years passed, we stopped badgering him. We were afraid he would tire of our curiosity and leave us.

Actually, he sometimes disappeared for several days and nights without forewarning or explanation. Did he go to see his family? His fiancée? His business associates? More likely he was hiding in some mountain cave nearby, or wandering aimlessly in the woods, a free man responsible to no one. But he always reappeared in the house of study before we had time to become worried.

One year I invited him to share our Passover meal. He thanked me effusively but insisted he had accepted a previous invitation. Whose?

"To tell you would not be good manners, right?" was all he said.

I had to acquiesce. But during the entire holiday he was not at the synagogue. In vain did I look for him in other places of worship; he was nowhere to be found. Then I had a startling thought: What if he had gone to celebrate the Seder in his own home. Could there be truth in what people were whispering about him? If not, why would he be so mysterious?

The day after Passover, I saw him sitting on his usual bench. Had he had a pleasant holiday? I asked.

"Yes," he said.

"Where?"

"Oh, not very far from here."

"Do I know the place?"

"No, I don't think so. At least, not yet."

"Could I go with you next time?"

"Of course, but you will need a proper invitation."

By that time people had begun to treat him as a madman. Even though he showed no signs of madness. He was not subject to irrational outbursts or abnormal impulses. He never caused scenes, showed no taste for violence and stayed away from disturbances. Rarely was he in anyone's way; he lived silently, as in a shell.

More than that: he was clearly an educated and well-read man. He spoke several languages and understood literature and art. One had the feeling that he had grown up surrounded by comfort and had attended the university of his choosing. But he admitted to nothing. Why did we think he was mad? Because we failed to understand his motivations? Because he had forsaken the glittering life of the city for a remote dusty village like ours? No, I thought, he is not mad, his presence in our midst was probably connected with some secret purpose binding him to us.

In the beginning I saw in him a *tzaddik* in disguise, a saintly sage whose mission it was to gather sparks and wandering souls to unite them with the original and sacred flame, the flame that links the Creator to His creation. Later, I don't know why, I found myself treating him like a prince belonging to the distant kingdom of the Ten Lost Tribes. One day, after a certain event, he would return to his castle. Then we would learn the truth. But it would be too late. The prince would never again visit our little town.

The event took place. Passover 1944 saw our synagogues closed, our houses of prayer and learning evacuated. A thousand burning questions troubled me, including: Where would Shmukler seek shelter? I tried in vain to get information. I questioned the other beggars, the other madmen. In the midst of chaos, they had been too busy to worry about Shmukler, who had vanished, leaving no trace. I too had so many problems of my own I could not afford to linger on his case.

But once again I found him. The first convoy was ready to leave the ghetto. I noticed Shmukler from afar: he was standing by himself, calm, serene, in control of his body and eyes. I don't recall whether he carried a suitcase or a bundle. I think neither; it was a bag belonging to the old woman shuffling along beside him. There was a smile on his face and even in his eyes.

It was as though he understood where they were taking him. He knew they were taking him home. Other victims were already waiting for him, over there, in the mysterious palace of the invisible king. He knew he would be riding a black steed, who would pull him higher and higher, until in the presence of the king he would point out the arsonists below. He would never see the town of my childhood again. That too he knew.

So, twenty-five years later, I ask you the question: How does one commemorate his death and that of an entire community? What must one say? How many candles should one light, how many prayers should one recite, and how many times? Perhaps someone knows the answer. I don't. I am still searching and I still do not know what one must do to keep alive the image of a town which seems more and more unreal to me each day.

That is why I describe and embellish it so often, and often more than it deserves. I did not know it in its ugliness but at its most exalted, as it appeared to a young Jew for whom its outlines fused with those of his imagination.

I was too young to be aware of insinuations in people's small-talk; I listened only to their prayers. I was too innocent to understand the hunger and misery of our beggars, the dilemmas faced by our dreamers, the tragedy of our madmen. Though I am less naïve now, I cannot help but remember them as I saw them then: creatures from paradise struck down by human malediction.

I see them still—and shall see them always—walking toward the station, heads bowed, their mouths twisted by thirst and grief. They walk and walk and never stop or rest, for the dead need no rest; they are tireless, the dead, and there can be no will powerful enough to impede their march. The Angel of Death himself is powerless, for they are stronger than he, stronger than anyone. All we can do is watch them walk and tell the story of their march, which is the story of an end, a story that has no end.

Their endless march seems to lead toward an encounter in time rather than space. An encounter with whom? So as not to offend them, someone should be waiting for them. Who? That does not matter. What matters is where: Sighet. No other place will do.

And that town they themselves invented they are now carrying farther and farther away, endowing it with a thousand names and a thousand faces. Look and you'll see: it follows them, and so do I, keeping my distance, afraid to come too close. I follow their footsteps and murmur psalms, then I say *Kaddish*, once, ten times, a hundred times. How many times, I ask you, how many times should one say *Kaddish* for the death of a community buried in ashes, how many times must one repeat it for the twenty-fifth anniversary of that death? I do not know, I shall never know. What I do know is that we shall have to invent new prayers for the body as well as for the soul. For whoever tells you that soul can attain greater heights than body, bid him hold his tongue, for he does not know what he is saying. He did not see the Jews of my town, the Jews of all the towns like mine; he did not see their bodies become light as fire, lighter than ashes, invading the sky and our memory, and God's.

DIALOGUES I

SINCE WHEN *are you here?*
Since yesterday.

Only since yesterday?
No. I've always been here. Almost as if I'd been born here.

Born? What a word to use in this place!
That's true of all words.

Still, you do use them, don't you?
Less and less.

Does it tire you to speak?
It's not that: words confine, when what I want is to escape.

Do you succeed?
Sometimes.

How?
Through images.

What images?
Of a life already lived.

When? Where?
At home. Before.

Then there was a before?
Yes. I think so. I hope so.

And you go back to it?
I think so. I hope so.

To do what?
To eat.

Is that all?
Yes. Eat and eat again. With my parents. The Shabbat meal. With friends, guests, beggars on their way through town. White bread, fish, vegetables. Eat slowly, very slowly. Chew. Relish the flavor. Fruit. Sweets. Lots and lots of them. From morning till night.

Is that all you think about?
That's all I can see.

And the future? Don't you ever think of the future?
Oh yes. Tonight's soup, tomorrow's dry bread: isn't that the future? In my thoughts, I've already swallowed the soup, I've already devoured the bread. There is no more future.

*

Who are you?
A number.

Your name?
Gone. Blown away. Into the sky. Look up there. The sky is black, black with names.

I cannot see the sky. The barbed wire is in my way.
But I can. I look at the barbed wire and I know that what
    I'm seeing is the sky.

You mean they have barbed wire up there too?
Of course.

And all that goes with it?
The lot.

*The tormentors? The executioners? The victims with
    neither strength nor desire to resist, to smile at the
    shadows?*
I'm telling you: it's just like here.

Then we are lost.
We alone?

*

How old are you?
Fifteen. Or more. Perhaps less. I don't know. And you?

I'm fifty.
I envy you. You look younger.

And you, you look older.
Anyway, we're both wrong. I'm convinced of it. I am
    fifty and you're fifteen. Do you mind?

*Not at all. You or I, it's all the same. Tell me: do you
    know who you are?*
No. Do you?

I don't.
Are you at least sure that you exist?

I'm not. Are you?
No, neither am I.

But our faces? What has happened to them?
They are masks. Loaned to him who has no face.

*

Are you asleep?
No. It's something else.

*Are you dreaming? With your eyes open? Letting your
imagination run wild? Trying to feel human and
fulfilled?*
I'm too weak for that.

Then what are you doing? Your eyes are wide open.
I'm playing.

You're what?
I'm playing a game of chess.

With whom?
I don't know.

Who's winning?
That too I don't know. I only know who's losing.

*

Hey, you there! You look like you're praying.
Not so.

Your lips keep moving.
A matter of habit, probably.

Did you use to pray that much?
That much. And even more.

What did you ask for in your prayers?
Nothing.

For pardon?
Maybe.

For knowledge?
Possibly.

Friendship?
Yes, friendship.

For a chance to defeat evil and be linked to what is good?
 For some certainty of living within truth or of—
 just—living?
Perhaps.

And you call that nothing?
Precisely. I call that nothing.

  *

Were you rich?
Very rich. Like a king.

What did your father do?
He was a merchant. He had to work hard.

I thought that rich people didn't work.
My father worked. From daybreak, late into the night.
 My mother helped him. We all helped, even the chil-
dren. We had no choice.

33

Then he wasn't rich.

Yes, he was. No beggar ever left us without first enjoying a good meal at our table, in our company. My mother would serve him first. During holidays our house would overflow with the poor: our guests of honor.

Where did you live?
In a palace. Spacious, immense. And beautiful. Luxurious. Unique.

How many rooms?
Three. No, four. We pushed each other a little, it didn't matter. There was no running water. Still, it was a palace.

Will you go back one day?
Never. The place is gone.

What will you do when all this is over?
Build a house and fill it with food. Then I'll invite all the poor of the earth to come share my meals. But . . .

Yes?
. . . but nobody will come, because all this will never be over.

*

Do you know you are like one possessed? You have only one thought, one wish: to eat to your heart's content.
I'm hungry.

It's not becoming to think of food all the time.
It's not becoming to be hungry all the time.

You mean to tell me nothing else counts?
There *is* nothing else.

And what about ideas? Ideals? All the great dreams of man imposing his will on the universe? The old man's joy of discovering at last the secret of the wait?
You may have them all for one crust of bread.

And God?
Let's not talk about God. Not here.

Could it be you no longer believe in Him?
I didn't say that.

Am I to understand your faith has not deserted you?
I didn't say that either. I said that I refuse to speak about God, here in this place. To say yes would be to lie. To say no—also. If need be, I would confront Him with an angry shout, a gesture, a murmur. But to make of Him—here—a theological topic, that I won't do! God—here—is the extra bowl of soup pushed at you or stolen from you, simply because the man ahead of you is either stronger or quicker than you. God—here—cannot be found in humble or grandiloquent phrases, but in a crust of bread . . .

Which you have had or are about to have?
. . . which you will never have.

*

Will you remember me?
I promise.

35

But how? You don't know who I am, not even I know that.

It doesn't matter: I shall remember my promise.

For a long time?

For as long as possible. All my life perhaps. But . . . why are you laughing?

So that you may remember my laughter as well as the look in my eyes.

You lie. You laugh because you are going mad.

Perfect. Remember my madness.

Tell me . . . am I the reason you're laughing?

You're not the only one, my boy, you're not the only one.

READINGS

Treblinka, Birkenau, Belsen, Buchenwald, Auschwitz, Mauthausen, Belzec, Ponar, Sobibor, Majdanek: somber capitals of a strange kingdom, immense and timeless, where Death, as sovereign, assumed the face of God as well as his attributes in heaven and on earth and even in the heart of man.

The time: 1941–1945. In the middle of the holocaust, a term implying the mystical dimension of the "concentrationary" phenomenon. Nazi Germany is collapsing under the weight of its evil, but for all that, the Jews will not win the war. Many will not see victory.

Written off and abandoned, no power will grant them protection. Their fate has no place on the agendas of the Big Three. Nor does it rouse the conscience of nations. Writers, artists, moralists: some are absorbed by their work, their immortality, others by the conflict in its totality. Everything proceeds as though the Jews did not exist, as though they existed no more. As though Auschwitz were but a peaceful town somewhere in Silesia. President Roosevelt refuses to bomb the railroad tracks leading to it. When consulted, Winston Churchill concurs in the refusal. Moscow condemns German atrocities perpetrated against civilian populations, but blankets in silence the massacre of

37

the Jews. On both sides, they are sacrificed in advance. People say: History will judge. Indeed. But it will judge without understanding. As for Adolf Hitler, he understands. Moreover, he is convinced that his adversaries themselves will be grateful to him for having resolved for them the eternal Jewish Question. Justice will be rendered him one day and he will be proclaimed the benefactor of humanity; he is persuaded of that.

A gigantic and efficient organization is already at work. Theoreticians, executives, guards, secretaries, typists, engineers and technicians of various kinds: all devote to it their energy and enthusiasm. For them, it is the great adventure, the ideal, the exhilarating rise of their star: they are taking part in the most profound mutation of all times, they are reconstructing humanity on new foundations. Thanks to them, this chosen but weakened people will sink into oblivion. The process is everywhere the same. All roads end in night.

Rejected by mankind, the condemned do not go so far as to reject it in turn. Their faith in history remains unshaken, and one may well wonder why. They do not despair. The proof: they persist in surviving—not only to survive, but to testify.

The victims elect to become witnesses.

On his way to the mass grave, the historian Simon Dubnow exhorts the Jews of Riga, his companions in misfortune: "Open your eyes and ears, remember every detail, every name, every sigh! The color of the clouds, the hissing of the wind in the trees, the executioner's every gesture: the one who survives must forget nothing!"

In Birkenau, a member of the Sonderkommando in charge of maintaining the furnaces, compiles, by the light of the flames, reports and detailed statistics for future generations.

Everywhere, at the very core of distress and death, young militants and wizened old men make notes, consign to paper events, anecdotes, impressions. Some are only children: David Rubinstein and Anne Frank.

Behind the walls of the Warsaw Ghetto, Emmanuel Ringelblum and his hundred scribes have but a single thought: to gather and bury as many documents as possible —so much suffering, so many trials must not be lost to History. Since European Jewry is doomed, it becomes imperative to at least preserve the scorched vestiges of its passing.

Poems, litanies, plays: to write them, Jews went without sleep, bartered their food for pencils and paper. They gambled with their fate. They risked their lives. No matter. They went on fitting together words and symbols. An instant before perishing in Auschwitz, in Bialistok, in Buna, dying men described their agony. In Buchenwald, I attended several "literary" evenings and listened to anonymous poets reciting verses I was too young to understand. They did not write them for me, for us, but for the others, those on the outside and those yet unborn.

There was then a veritable passion to testify for the future, against death and oblivion, a passion conveyed by every possible means of expression.

Terse documents. Precisely kept ledgers of horrors. Accounts told with childlike artlessness. What they have in common is their desire to tear from the clutches of night the life and death of what was once a flourishing, vibrant community before it became a hunted pack at bay. Haunting, terrifying, they waver between scream and silent anger. Established facts, known episodes, examined and re-examined, yet endlessly astounding, episodes which are comic and therefore all the more harrowing: one always thinks one knows this or that aspect of the holocaust. Wrong: everything remains to be discovered. Reading certain books by authors who do not know each other, one wonders: they describe the same scenes, the same partings. It all begins and it all ends the same way. It has all been said, yet all remains to be said.

Autobiographical accounts or imagined texts, the principal character remains the camp or the ghetto, each with its diminishing population devoured by time or death.

The ghetto with its ghosts, its gravediggers, the empty, glassy or demented stares of its children. The inside of a nightmare one gets used to, and even very quickly: in a single night, a single hour, one acquires knowledge and wisdom. The child discovers the old man within himself. Overnight, familiar patterns and concepts give way. To be replaced by new ones. Soon accepted. One loves, invokes the purity and irreducibility of love, celebrates marriages and religious holidays. One sings, hides, deceives and mocks oneself. One begs for a potato, a shred of consolation. One sees oneself as other and elsewhere. And what if tomorrow one dies of hunger, of illness, of exhaustion or simply of hope—yes, hope.

Crazed with pain, tortured, an eight-year-old cries out: "I want to steal, I want to eat, I want to be German.

So I can eat, eat without shame, and sleep, sleep without fear." He dies without eating. Other children mature too early, succumb to the cold, to the anguish of seeing their parents humiliated and beaten. Some become targets for soldiers who as good warriors must practice their aim.

And then there are the camps. And the fear they arouse in the inhabitants of the ghettos. The children are taken first. Then come the old, the jobless, the sick, the resigned, all those who do not possess a working permit, either yellow, red or green, stamped by the military, the police or the German employer. Anyway, one never knows which color is the right one.

Ultimately, nobody believes in permits or pledges any more. Here and there, young people arm themselves or join the partisans in the woods. Here and there, they build subterranean shelters, fortified bunkers, lines of defense. Here and there, they prepare an insurrection to teach humanity and history a lesson they hardly deserve. The one in Warsaw will not be forgotten. There were others less well known. And yet, every revolt had its poet, every massacre its historian. How many documents still lie buried at the bottom of how many pits? One day they will be discovered. For the moment, every account from every ghetto is valid for all. The same anger animates them. Will there come a day when it will be appeased?

Some witnesses answer no. They value their anger and cling to it. It constitutes their link with a world gone by. In their rage, they spare neither the living nor the dead. To better illustrate the evil which dominated all levels of the "concentrationary" kingdom, they challenge even the victims by reproaching them for their docility. That evil had an absolute coefficient is beyond doubt. At Auschwitz one breathed contempt and indignity: a crust of bread was worth more than divine promises, a bowl of soup transformed a sensitive human being into a wild animal. Principles, disciplines and feelings only feebly resisted the implacable laws of Majdanek.

A killer, for his amusement, simulated the execution of a Jew; he knocked him unconscious and fired a shot into the air. Opening his eyes, the Jew saw his killer bent over him, sneering: "You thought you could escape us by dying? Even in the other world we are the masters!"

Anecdote which contains a part of truth: in dealing with the victims, in an effort to break their morale before annihilating them, the executioners assumed the role of God. They alone could, by decree, proclaim the limits of good and evil. Their idiosyncrasies were law and so were their whims. They were above morality, above truth.

Prisoners of such a system, many deportees chose the easy path of abdication. How is one to judge them? I do not. I cannot condemn anyone who failed to withstand trials and temptations. Guilty or not, the ghetto police, the *kapos*, may plead extenuating circumstances. They arouse pity more than contempt. The weak, the cowardly, all those who sold their soul to live another day, another anxious night, I prefer to include them in the category of victims. More than the others, they need forgiveness. More and in other ways than their companions, they deserve compassion and charity. Their guilt reflects on their tormentors.

Still, I sometimes read books presented as evidence for the prosecution. Their authors are harsh, their judgments devoid of compassion. Whether their words hurt or shock matters little: they will be heard. Of necessity fragmentary, they do not reflect the whole but are part of it. In fact, this can serve as a general rule: every witness expresses only his own truth, in his own name. To convey the truth of the holocaust in its totality, it is not enough to have listened to the survivors, one must find a way to add the silence left behind by millions of unknowns. That silence can have no interpreter. One cannot conceive of the holocaust except as a mystery, begotten by the dead.

We question today, and will continue to wonder for a long time, how such crimes and horrors could have been committed. We shall never know. Or why one people chose murder and another martyrdom. We shall never know why. All questions pertaining to Auschwitz lead to anguish. Whether or not the death of one million children has meaning, either way man is negated and condemned. Auschwitz defies the novelist's language, the historian's analysis, the vision of the prophet. Survivors and witnesses have done their best to describe their experiences, yet their writings have perhaps no substantial relationship with what they have seen and lived through. They have written because they could not do otherwise: after all, one needed to lift the tombstone, however slightly, and grope one's way out of the night. By speaking out, they have forced us to see that the mystery endures. Which, if it means anything, means defeat. In its presence, words ring hollow. In its shadow, we may well be impostors. Will there be a day when we will know what was the reality of Auschwitz?

Perhaps Auschwitz never existed, except for those who left there, beneath the ashes, a part of their future in pledge.

The Talmud relates: when the Temple in Jerusalem was set on fire, the priests interrupted the sacred services, climbed on the roof and spoke to God: "We were not able to safeguard Your dwelling, therefore we surrender to You its keys." And they hurled them toward heaven.

Sometimes I think that somewhere the sanctuary is still burning and that the survivors are its priests. But they are keeping the keys.

SNAPSHOTS

A JEW, on his knees, is digging a grave. You imagine him dazed, barely conscious. His blackened face, dimly seen, is blurred, half-obscured by night. You can see his parents, his brothers; broken, twisted masks of clay. From behind, arms crossed, legs spread wide, the killers in uniform calmly observe the digging man. Relaxed and jovial, they exchange remarks. They laugh.

*

An old woman, a yellow star on her chest, turns to cast a last bewildered glance at the station before disappearing inside the train already carrying a hundred tangled anonymous bodies. We see her still, leaning on the steps, but we are no longer looking at her: her shadow is what we see. No, not even her shadow.

*

And this faceless corpse, what country and what landscape did he choose as a setting for his abdication? Discreetly he has turned his head away. Did shame for his

45

fellow men compel him to cover his eyes with his shabby vest? He had reached the end, he wanted to see nothing more. He had seen it all, measured it all. He died blind. Here he is, lying lifeless across a pile of stones, his fist brandished as though to chase away some distant foe. Look closely at his feet: his right shoe is missing. And the left foot? A bone, without a trace of skin.

These snapshots, taken by German officers and soldiers, collectors of exotic souvenirs, appear in various albums devoted to the holocaust. Examine them and you will forget who you are. You will no longer want to know. Nothing will be important any more. You will have glimpsed an abyss you would rather not have uncovered. Too late.

Leafing through these collections of photographs, you feel yourself sinking, numbed and dizzy, into a bottomless and glacial night. Fellow humans seem to recede, your ties with them more fragile. But the very next day, there you are, facing those pages again.

Deep down I know that every eye staring into mine cuts off the new branch of a tree and adds yet another stain to the sun. I know that every image robs me of another reason for hope. And still my fingers turn the pages, and the shriveled bodies, the gaping twisted mouths, their screams lost in space, continue to follow one another. Then the anguish clutching me, choking me, grows darker and darker; it crushes me: with all these corpses before my eyes, I am afraid to stumble over my own.

At every page, in front of every image, I stop to catch my breath. And I tell myself: This is the end, they have reached the last limit; what follows can only be less horrible; surely it is impossible to invent suffering more naked, cruelty more refined. Moments later I admit my error: I underestimated the assassins' ingenuity. The progression into the inhuman transcends the exploration of the human. Evil, more than good, suggests infinity.

How can you explain the masochistic urge that impels you to leave opened before you the book of a past in shrouds but without a grave? Above all, there is the thirst for knowledge, the desire to understand. The tales about atrocities, the survivors are the ones who read them. So as to decipher, belatedly, the truth that had eluded them. So as to know all there is to know about the event that mutilated them. Because, in fact, they still do not understand what happened. And how—and why—they were spared. By delving into documents and diagrams, studies and memoirs, they hope to gain a new perspective on themselves, and perhaps beyond. Photographs are even more evocative than words, any words; they are ruthless, definitive, precise. Fascinated by the memory they imprison, the survivor studies them to rediscover an image of himself he had thought extinct: his own way of saying *Kaddish*, with his eyes rather than his mouth. That mouth—surely it is guilty of too many wrongs: remaining silent when it ought to have spoken, speaking when there was nothing left to say. More faithful, the eyes are better witnesses: they have forgotten nothing.

Seen in profile, the prisoner seems strangely serene. One might think him seated, were it not for the belt tightened around his neck, its other end fastened to a pipe screwed into the ceiling. The hanged man could not have chosen a more fitting or symbolic place: the latrines. Hereby elevated to courtroom, where the suicide has come to deliver a sentence of death.

And more. Under a dull gray sky, in the very middle of a wheat field, five men topple like stalks of wheat under the scythe. Another page: an ageless mother, livid with terror, grimly clutches her child to protect it from the oncoming bullets. Behind her, a soldier, his face an impassive blank, pulls the trigger. And so she falls, the mother, as does her child, they fall and fall, there is no end to their falling.

Don't stop. Not yet. The next page shows you children with bloated heads like old men, and old men with childlike emaciated bodies. Another displays pregnant women hanging from trees, motionless; causing neither leaves nor wind to tremble, unleashing no storm.

And still the eye wants to see, the finger to turn the pages. The scenes follow and resemble one another, and suddenly their similarity strikes you like a whip: you are looking at the same Jew murdered six million times by one killer, always the same.

Spellbound, dazed, your eyes keep looking. You have shattered the mirror, you are on the other side. Go on, turn the pages, drink in the night they reveal, open yourself to the fixed smiles endlessly dying, the countless arms stretched toward you, capture those wandering gazes that belong to the dead. And then, who cares if, seized with rage and remorse, you spit on this world which was theirs and still is yours.

So, go on. There is more, much more. The pictures spin, become a kaleidoscope and send you back into infinity.

Come on, don't give up. You haven't seen it all; you haven't
seen anything. Wait: after this ghetto, you'll visit another,
bigger, smaller, closer to hell. Then you will see the forests
where the mass executions were held. The graves, the
stakes. The fathers and sons who spoke or remained silent
before tumbling into the trench. The departures and ar-
rivals. The railway stations, the arbitrary selections. The
musicians, the fires. The hunger, the fear, the plague, the
shame, the end. Names file past you, pay no attention.
Hungarian towns, Polish ghettos, Lithuanian cemeteries, it's
everywhere the same. The fear is everywhere and the hunger and the shame and the end. Go on.

Who is this old man and how dare he defy his torturers?
They are cutting off his beard, they are hurting him deliberately. All of them want to take part. Yet he does not
complain. Does not moan. Silent and proud, his head held
high, he looks straight into their eyes. You're impressed
by his dignity, aren't you? Why, he is provoking them!
He is mad, they will kill him! Doesn't he know? He seems
to be mocking them. I study him more closely. His features
seem familiar. A hunch. Followed by a complicated, tor-
tuous investigation. No, my memory has not deceived me.
Yes, it is my grandfather.

Another image forever etched into my mind. A small
Jewish boy, his hands above his head like a soldier giving
himself up to the enemy after a fierce battle. Fear has just
overtaken him. His cap, too big for his head, hides his
forehead and ears but not the two black braziers that are
his eyes. Does he see the soldiers encircling him? The
snipers lying in wait? How many are they? Ten, a hundred,
a hundred thousand? Armed with revolvers, rifles, sub-
machine guns. All the German warriors, from all fronts,

far and near, have converged here for the sole purpose of slaughtering this one little Jewish boy with knowing eyes, out of breath, and clearly lacking both strength and desire to resist.

A ghetto scene: a fighter jumps from a window, a living torch, pursued by flame-throwers. In the street below, Germans and Poles, military and civilians, find the spectacle interesting.

And from Treblinka—or is it Birkenau, Ponar, Majdanek?—this image which one day will burst inside me like a sharp call to madness: Jewish mothers, naked, leading their children, also naked, to the sacrifice. You stare at them so hard that in the end you see them advancing through an immense flowering field toward an altar red with blood, then you see them suspended halfway between heaven and earth, startled angels condemned to silence. Look at the women, some still young and beautiful, their frightened children well-behaved. Others, older and without illusions, are weary, so weary. And here they are, modestly trying to hide their femininity. The children respectfully avert their gaze. And you, what are you doing? Go ahead, go on, snatch a flower, offer it to the mothers in exchange for their children—what are you waiting for? Hurry up, quickly, grab a child and run, run as fast as your legs will carry you, faster than the wind, run while there's still time, before you are blinded by the smoke . . .

. . . But motionless and mute, there you remain, like myself, in front of these images that men like you and me took pleasure in consigning to film, to be shown later, back home, to boring guests and admiring cousins.

The fingers turn page after page and your eyes meet again the eyes that burn them. On the far bank of the river, the sun, having warmed the earth, sinks into a deep red twilight flecked with gold. And what if the holocaust were nothing but a nightmare, a parenthesis?

The world has remained world. Men have not changed nor have they learned anything: perhaps there was nothing to learn. Love, vanity of vanities, jealousies: life goes on. Vacations, automobiles, demonstrations: one follows the trends. Yesterday's myths give way to today's prefabricated heroes and idols. Scientists succeed artists. On all continents, nations, large and small, get ready to kill one another. Business tycoons make deals, and politicians speeches. Profiteers worry about their reputations, and artists about their art. As for me, I too like to attend a good concert or smile back at a pretty girl. I bless bread and sanctify the wine, and no one is happier than I when, under my pen, words fall into place, fit into a design and create the illusion that they are leading somewhere.

In truth, I know where they lead. To where there are no words. To the mysterious forests where fathers and sons, Jews already marked by the executioner, always the same, tell each other a story, always the same. To where women with dark dilated pupils, violated and drunk with pain, escort their children to the altar and beyond.

Then there arises from the very depths of my being an irresistible desire to let everything go. To throw away the pen, burn all bridges and start to run and curse and leave the present far behind. To seek the moment that gave birth to these images, and never again to hear the laughter, and the moaning of the wind whipped by the shadows, always the same shadows.

DIALOGUES II

Are you *angry with me?*
Sometimes. A little.

Because I didn't suffer like you?
Because you were here and did nothing.

What could we have done?
Cry. Scream. Break the conspiracy of silence.

We didn't know.
Not true. Everybody knew. Nobody bothers to deny
that any more.

All right, we knew. But we didn't believe.
In spite of all the proof, the diagrams, the confidential
reports?

*Because of them. Don't you see? They were so horrible,
we couldn't believe them.*
You should have.

*And you, would you have believed them? What's more,
you who lived through this experience, do you
really believe, today, that it took place?*
No. But . . .

Yes?

. . . with me, it's different. Sometimes I wonder if I still have the right to say "I."

*

Here he is! That's him! Quick, grab him!
What are you talking about?

That's him, I tell you! He is dangerous, he must be put away!
But what do you want from him? What has he done?

Nothing, but . . .
He's done nothing? And you want to lock him up, punish him?

Just lock him up. He is capable of anything; he knows too much about man and his planet. He must be protected; we must be protected. If he starts talking, we're done for. We must do everything to keep him quiet!
But he hasn't said anything yet, has he?

All the more reason to lock him up right away while there's still time! Lock him up with the madmen without memory, without future! As long as he is free, I feel threatened.
Did you ever speak to him?

Never. But he spoke to me.
What did he tell you?

He asked my forgiveness.
That's all?

You don't think that's enough? He was joking, I know. I'm the one who should ask his forgiveness. I don't dare; I'm afraid of his voice, of his eyes. In his presence, I feel cold. I become his secret, the very one he means to carry into his grave. He frightens me; I don't dare move or breathe. Or even look. My head hits the wall, and the wall is he, is you—and I, where am I? Who am I? He alone knows and that is his vengeance. I am telling you: he is dangerous! Help!

*

You don't look well, you really don't.
Oh, I'll be all right.

Are you sad?
Could be. Nothing serious.

You should see yourself.
I believe you.

You can't go on like this.
What do you want me to do?

How should I know? Look around you. The trees in bloom. The shop windows. The pretty girls. What the hell, let yourself go. I promise you that after . . .
After? Did you say: after? Meaning what?

*

Tell me something.
Anything in particular?

54

That you like me.
I like you.

That you missed me.
I missed you.

That you love me.
I love you.

That you want to live with me.
I want to live with you.

Does that frighten you?
Yes.

I am frightened only when you're away.
So am I.

Then stay with me.
I'll try.

And you'll speak to me?
I'll try.

You don't trust words?
Worse. I've lost all connection with words.

But I am afraid of your silences.
So am I.

As soon as you stop speaking, you stop seeing.
No, only then do I begin to see.

*

Do you remember me?
No.

55

We were neighbors.
Possibly.

We were friends.
When?

Before.
Oh yes, I remember.

We went to the same school, dreamed the same dreams, admired the same teachers.
Oh, yes, I do remember. We thought of becoming rabbis.

What are you doing now? I am a sculptor. And you?
I write.

The way you say that . . .
What do you expect? Millions of human beings had to die so that you might become a sculptor and I, a storyteller.

*

I'd like to ask you a question, only it might embarrass you.
Go ahead. Ask.

How did you manage to sleep?
Where? There?

Yes, there.
My dear lady, it was easy: I counted corpses. There were lots of them. They all looked alike in the dark—including myself. I would get mixed up. Then I would have to start over and over again: there was always one too many. Sleep was the only way to

rid myself of the last intruder. But why do you want to know?

Oh, I am just curious.
Too bad. I thought you had trouble sleeping.

*

You look sad, or sick.
I'm not.

You feel all right? You have enough to eat? There's nothing wrong with you?
I have no complaints.

You are not troubled by other people's happiness? Or by the innocence of children?
I like happiness and I love children.

Then why do you tell them sad stories?
My stories are not sad. The children will tell you that.

But they make one cry, don't they?
No, they do not make one cry.

Don't tell me they make one laugh!
I won't. I'll only say they make one dream.

*

Play with me, will you?
All right.

I am the messenger.
Hello, messenger.

57

I am powerful and generous.
Bravo, messenger.

I wish you well.
Hail to the messenger!

*What is your dearest, your most secret wish? Tell me
and it will come true.*
You're a nice messenger.

So? What is your wish?
Oh yes, here it is: grant me that I may meet someone like
you.

*

Are you there?
I am here, son.

It's so dark. I'm trembling. I have a fever. I'm afraid.
I'm here.

Are we alone, you and I?
I think so.

Would you do something for me?
Naturally, son.

Sing for me.
At this hour?

You refuse?
But we might wake the whole house, the whole street . . .

*Never mind. I want you to sing. For me. For yourself as
well. You promised me. When you sing, we are not
alone. It is still dark and I'm still afraid, but it*

doesn't matter, you understand, the fear no longer comes from outside but from your song, from your words, it comes from myself . . . are you there?
Yes, son. We are all here.

THE WATCH

FOR MY BAR MITZVAH, I remember, I had received a magnificent gold watch. It was the customary gift for the occasion, and was meant to remind each boy that henceforth he would be held responsible for his acts before the Torah and its timeless laws.

But I could not keep my gift. I had to part with it the very day my native town became the pride of the Hungarian nation by chasing from its confines every single one of its Jews. The glorious masters of our municipality were jubilant: they were rid of us, there would be no more kaftans on the streets. The local newspaper was brief and to the point: from now on, it would be possible to state one's place of residence without feeling shame.

The time was late April, 1944.

In the early morning hours of that particular day, after a sleepless night, the ghetto was changed into a cemetery and its residents into gravediggers. We were digging feverishly in the courtyard, the garden, the cellar, consigning to the earth, temporarily we thought, whatever remained of the belongings accumulated by several generations, the sorrow and reward of long years of toil.

My father took charge of the jewelry and valuable papers. His head bowed, he was silently digging near the barn. Not far away, my mother, crouched on the damp ground, was burying the silver candelabra she used only on Shabbat eve; she was moaning softly, and I avoided her eyes. My sisters burrowed near the cellar. The youngest, Tziporah, had chosen the garden, like myself. Solemnly shoveling, she declined my help. What did she have to hide? Her toys? Her school notebooks? As for me, my only possession was my watch. It meant a lot to me. And so I decided to bury it in a dark, deep hole, three paces away from the fence, under a poplar tree whose thick, strong foliage seemed to provide a reasonably secure shelter.

All of us expected to recover our treasures. On our return, the earth would give them back to us. Until then, until the end of the storm, they would be safe.

Yes, we were naïve. We could not foresee that the very same evening, before the last train had time to leave the station, an excited mob of well-informed friendly neighbors would be rushing through the ghetto's wide-open houses and courtyards, leaving not a stone or beam unturned, throwing themselves upon the loot.

Twenty years later, standing in our garden, in the middle of the night, I remember the first gift, also the last, I ever received from my parents. I am seized by an irrational, irresistible desire to see it, to see if it is still there in the same spot, and if defying all laws of probability, it has survived—like me—by accident, not knowing how or why. My curiosity becomes obsession. I think neither of my father's money nor of my mother's candlesticks. All that matters in this town is my gold watch and the sound of its ticking.

Despite the darkness, I easily find my way in the garden. Once more I am the bar mitzvah child; here is the barn, the fence, the tree. Nothing has changed. To my left, the path leading to the Slotvino Rebbe's house. The Rebbe, though, had changed: the burning bush burned itself out and there is nothing left, not even smoke. What could he possibly have hidden the day we went away? His phylacteries? His prayer shawl? The holy scrolls inherited from his famous ancestor Rebbe Meirl of Premishlan? No, probably not even that kind of treasure. He had taken everything along, convinced that he was thus protecting not only himself but his disciples as well. He was proved wrong, the wonder rabbi.

But I mustn't think of him, not now. The watch, I must think of the watch. Maybe it was spared. Let's see, three steps to the right. Stop. Two forward. I recognize the place. Instinctively, I get ready to re-enact the scene my memory recalls. I fall on my knees. What can I use to dig? There is a shovel in the barn; its door is never locked. But by groping around in the dark I risk stumbling and waking the people sleeping in the house. They would take me for a marauder, a thief, and hand me over to the police. They might even kill me. Never mind, I'll have to manage without a shovel. Or any other tool. I'll use my hands, my nails. But it is difficult; the soil is hard, frozen, it resists as if determined to keep its secret. Too bad, I'll punish it by being the stronger.

Feverishly, furiously, my hands claw the earth, impervious to cold, fatigue and pain. One scratch, then another. No matter. Continue. My nails inch ahead, my fingers dig in, I bear down, my every fiber participates in the task. Little by little the hole deepens. I must hurry. My forehead touches the ground. Almost. I break out in a cold sweat, I am drenched, delirious. Faster, faster. I shall rip the earth from end to end, but I must know. Nothing can stop or frighten me. I'll go to the bottom of my fear, to the bottom of night, but I will know.

What time is it? How long have I been here? Five minutes, five hours? Twenty years. This night was defying time. I was laboring to exhume not an object but time itself, the soul and memory of that time. Nothing could be more urgent, more vital.

Suddenly a shiver goes through me. A sharp sensation, like a bite. My fingers touch something hard, metallic, rectangular. So I have not been digging in vain. The garden is spinning around me, over me. I stand up to catch my breath. A moment later, I'm on my knees again. Cautiously, gently I take the box from its tomb. Here it is, in the palm of my hand: the last relic, the only remaining symbol of everything I had loved, of everything I had been. A voice inside me warns: Don't open it, it contains nothing but emptiness, throw it away and run. I cannot heed the warning; it is too late to turn back. I need to know, either way. A slight pressure of my thumb and the box opens. I stifle the cry rising in my throat: the watch is there. Quick, a match. And another. Fleetingly, I catch a glimpse of it. The pain is blinding: could this thing, this object, be my gift, my pride? My past? Covered with dirt and rust, crawling with worms, it is unrecognizable, revolting. Unable to move, wondering what to do, I remain staring at it with the disgust one feels for love betrayed or a body debased. I am angry with myself for having yielded to curiosity. But disappointment gives way to profound pity: the watch too lived through war and holocaust, the kind reserved for watches perhaps. In its way, it too is a survivor, a ghost infested with humiliating sores and obsolete memories. Suddenly I feel the urge to carry it to my lips, dirty as it is, to kiss and console it with my tears, as one might console a living being, a sick friend returning from far away and requiring much kindness and rest, especially rest.

I touch it, I caress it. What I feel, besides compassion, is a strange kind of gratitude. You see, the men I had believed to be immortal had vanished into fiery clouds. My teachers, my friends, my guides had all deserted me. While this thing, this nameless, lifeless thing had survived for the sole purpose of welcoming me on my return and providing an epilogue to my childhood. And there awakens in me a desire to confide in it, to tell it my adventures, and in exchange, listen to its own. What had happened in my absence: who had first taken possession of my house, my bed? Or rather, no; our confidences could wait for another time, another place: Paris, New York, Jerusalem. But first I would entrust it to the best jeweler in the world, so that the watch might recover its luster, its memory of the past.

It is growing late. The horizon is turning a deep red. I must go. The tenants will soon be waking, they will come down to the well for water. No time to lose. I stuff the watch into my pocket and cross the garden. I enter the courtyard. From under the porch a dog barks. And stops at once: he knows I am not a thief, anything but a thief. I open the gate. Halfway down the street I am overcome by violent remorse: I have just committed my first theft.

I turn around, retrace my steps through courtyard and garden. Again I find myself kneeling, as at Yom Kippur services, beneath the poplar. Holding my breath, my eyes refusing to cry, I place the watch back into its box, close the cover, and my first gift once more takes refuge deep inside the hole. Using both hands, I smoothly fill in the earth to remove all traces.

Breathless and with pounding heart, I reach the still deserted street. I stop and question the meaning of what I have just done. And find it inexplicable.

In retrospect, I tell myself that probably I simply wanted to leave behind me, underneath the silent soil, a reflection of my presence. Or that somehow I wanted to transform my watch into an instrument of delayed vengeance: one day, a child would play in the garden, dig near the tree and stumble upon a metal box. He would thus learn that his parents were usurpers, and that among the inhabitants of his town, once upon a time, there had been Jews and Jewish children, children robbed of their future.

The sun was rising and I was still walking through the empty streets and alleys. For a moment I thought I heard the chanting of schoolboys studying Talmud; I also thought I heard the invocations of Hasidim reciting morning prayers in thirty-three places at once. Yet above all these incantations, I heard distinctly, but as though coming from far away, the tick-tock of the watch I had just buried in accordance with Jewish custom. It was, after all, the very first gift that a Jewish child had once been given for his very first celebration.

Since that day, the town of my childhood has ceased being just another town. It has become the face of a watch.

STORIES

A DISCIPLE CAME TO SEE Rebbe Pinhas of Koretz.

"Help me, Master," he said. "My distress is great; make it disappear. The world is filled with anguish and sadness. Men are not men. I have no faith in them, or in myself. I have faith in nothing. What shall I do, Rebbe, what shall I do?"

"Go and study. It's the only remedy I know."

"Woe unto me, I cannot even study," said the disciple. "So strong are my doubts, so all-pervasive, that they prevent me from studying. I open the Talmud and contemplate it. For weeks, months on end, I remain riveted to the same page. I cannot go further, not even by a step, not even by a line. What can I do, Rebbe, what can I do?"

When a Jew can provide no answer, he at least has a story to tell. And so Rebbe Pinhas of Koretz replied: "Know that what is happening to you also happened to me. When I was your age I stumbled over the same difficulties. I too was filled with questions and doubts. About the Creator and His creation. I too could not advance. I tried study, prayer, meditation. In vain. Fasting, penitence, silence. In vain. My doubts remained doubts, my questions remained open. Impossible to proceed. Then, one day, I learned that Rebbe Israel Baal Shem-Tov would be coming to our town. Curiosity led me to the house where he was praying. When I entered he was finishing the *Amida*. He turned around and the intensity in his eyes overwhelmed me. I knew he was not looking at me alone, yet I knew that I was less alone. Suddenly, without a word, I was able to go home, open the Talmud and plunge into my studies once more.

"You see," said Rebbe Pinhas of Koretz to his disciple, "the questions remained questions, my doubts were still as heavy with anguish, but I was able to continue."

*

Like all Jewish children of my town, I had to prepare a speech for my bar mitzvah, the ceremony which at thirteen would mark my acceptance by the community as a full member.

A few days before the event, I went to see my Rebbe and pleaded with him not to attend: "Try to understand, I will not dare open my mouth in your presence. Whatever new insights I may have, I have from you. Whatever I could say, you already know. And better than I. To speak with you present would be like playing teacher in front of my teacher."

He was a gentle man, fond of solitude. That is why it surprised me when he refused my request: "You want to exclude me from your celebration? I am sorry, but I shall be there." But seeing my agitation, he quickly added: "Later you will teach, you will communicate what you are now acquiring from me and others like me. I shall no longer be here to listen. But remember: I don't ask the storyteller to play the role of master; all I ask is that he fulfill his duty as messenger and witness."

To the astonishment of my parents and friends, I went through the ceremony without a speech.

*

This is the story of a ghetto that stopped living, and of a beadle who lost his mind.

It was the beadle's custom to rush to the synagogue each morning, to ascend the bimah and shout first with pride, and then with anger: "I have come to inform you, Master of the Universe, that we are here."

Then came the first massacre, followed by many others. The beadle somehow always emerged unscathed. As soon as he could, he would run to the synagogue, and pounding his fist on the lectern, would shout at the top of his voice: "You see, Lord, we are still here."

After the last massacre, he found himself all alone in the deserted synagogue. The last living Jew, he climbed the bimah one last time, stared at the Ark and whispered with infinite gentleness: "You see? I am still here."

He stopped briefly before continuing in his sad, almost toneless voice: "But You, where are You?"

*

They called him the madman, the ghetto madman. The starving gave him a crust of bread, a few potato peels. He amused and distracted them. As for the killers, they seemed to spare him. The convoys came and went, but he was left behind. People asked:

"How do you manage to escape the roundups?"

"A very important person is protecting me."

"And who is he?"

"The Council Chairman himself. I went to see him and told him that no community could survive without its madman. 'If you kill me, or allow me to be killed, you will take my place; you will be me.'"

Then the argument became pointless: there was no more community.

*

In a macabre display of humor, the killers informed the ghetto dwellers that ten hostages were to be hanged in reprisal for the execution of Haman and his sons, two thousand years earlier, in the Kingdom of Ahasuerus, as related in the Book of Esther.

Among the hostages, all bearing the name of Mordecai, after Esther's uncle, there was one poor man, a water-carrier by trade. He was the only one to go to the scaffold laughing. He was roaring with laughter.

"Have you gone crazy?"

"What an idea! Of course not!" he replied, shrieking with laughter.

"You are not afraid to die?"

"Afraid? Scared out of my wits!"

"Then why are you laughing?"

"One thing has nothing to do with the other." And he explained to the executioners: "Today I am Mordecai, the water-carrier. But tomorrow! Tomorrow I'll be Mordecai the Martyr, Mordecai the Saint; and him you'll never hang, never."

And he laughed. And there were no tears in his eyes.

*

Having concluded that human suffering was beyond endurance, a certain Rebbe went up to heaven and knocked at the Messiah's gate.

"Why are you taking so long?" he asked him. "Don't you know mankind is expecting you?"

"It's not me they are expecting," answered the Messiah. "Some are waiting for good health and riches. Others for serenity and knowledge. Or peace in the home and happiness. No, it's not me they are awaiting."

At this point, they say, the Rebbe lost patience and cried: "So be it! If you have but one face, may it remain in shadow! If you cannot help men, all men, resolve their problems, all their problems, even the most insignificant, then stay where you are, as you are. If you still have not guessed that you are bread for the hungry, a voice for the old man without heirs, sleep for those who dread night, if you have not understood all this and more: that every wait is a wait for you, then you are telling the truth: indeed, it is not you that mankind is waiting for."

The Rebbe came back to earth, gathered his disciples and forbade them to dispair:

"And now the true waiting begins."

*

Yesterday a beautiful young girl of exemplary behavior saw twilight approaching through the window as if to take possession of her. Her heart began to pound. She turned to her father, who was quietly reading his paper.

"I love you very much, Father," she said. "You know I do, don't you?"

"Of course," he answered, absorbed in his reading. "You're adorable. I am proud of you."

She turned to look at her mother, who was setting the table. "You, too, Mother, I love you very much. I haven't said this very often; it wasn't necessary. But know that it is true."

Her mother looked at her, astonished. "I should hope so! A daughter should love her parents. We, too, we love you; you're all we have." And, looking pleased with herself, she went on arranging the plates and forks and knives, not to mention the napkins.

The young girl thought of the boy she was to marry and she was overcome by sorrow. "You, we. We will conquer evil, re-create the world, have children, and I will love them, I will love them with all my strength, as I will also love the children we shall never have."

In the street below, cloaked in darkness, a stranger crossed the street, stared up at a house with tightly drawn curtains, and slowly walked away.

"You, too, stranger," the young girl whispered. "I make you a gift of my love. May your steps lead you toward a desired destination and not toward exile. May your hope free you from the fear which gave it birth. May the love inside you not kill the joy, may the joy inside you become haven and not prison."

She spoke to him until he turned the corner. Then, in a voice tinged with neither reproach nor regret, she cried:

"What am I to do, dear God, what am I to do? I love everybody, it's only myself I cannot love."

And the young girl, both virtuous and beautiful, threw herself out of the window.

*

One of the Just Men came to Sodom, determined to save its inhabitants from sin and punishment. Night and day he walked the streets and markets preaching against greed and theft, falsehood and indifference. In the beginning, people listened and smiled ironically. Then they stopped listening: he no longer even amused them. The killers went on killing, the wise kept silent, as if there were no Just Man in their midst.

One day a child, moved by compassion for the unfortunate preacher, approached him with these words: "Poor stranger. You shout, you expend yourself body and soul; don't you see that it is hopeless?"

"Yes, I see," answered the Just Man.

"Then why do you go on?"

"I'll tell you why. In the beginning, I thought I could change man. Today, I know I cannot. If I still shout today, if I still scream, it is to prevent man from ultimately changing me."

THE VIOLIN

Like most Jewish parents of the *shtetl*, mine wanted their son to study the violin. Not as a profession, God forbid, nor as a hobby. Simply as part of my education. Like the Talmud. Or Latin. It made a good impression. And it certainly couldn't hurt.

Without being overly enthusiastic, I was willing to try. I thought: What was good enough for King David will be good enough for me. Still there was the problem of finding a suitable instructor among the several in our town. Some were even ready to come to our house, except that we had no room. And then the neighbors might have raised understandable objections. To study with Miss Tudos was not a good idea either. Not only did she live too far, she was a woman. What would people say?

Finally, after many inquiries, my father found the ideal instructor in the person of a police captain quartered at the station nearby. I only had to cross the street.

Out of friendship for my father, he agreed to teach me without fee. Three lessons a week to begin with. Then a lesson a day, so that in a few years I could give my first concert—this was mentioned right away—on a Saturday evening at the Borsher Rebbe's during the traditional ceremony of escorting the Shabbat on its weekly journey into exile.

So I was given a second-hand violin, and the captain told my father he was expecting me.

It was a Sunday afternoon. The guard let me in, saluting as though I were an officer. I did not return his salute. I had my hands full: one was holding the violin, the other a bottle of *cuika*—a gift from my father. But even with my hands free I would not have known what to do: no one had ever taught me how a bashful little Jewish boy was to respond when saluted by a gigantic police sergeant.

The captain, seated at his desk, his knees crossed, welcomed me with a laugh. "Come closer. Don't be scared. Let me look at you. So you're our new Paganini."

"No, sir," I said, not knowing what he was talking about.

"How stupid of me," he continued. "How can you be Paganini when you're a Jew? No, you will be our Heifetz."

I knew as little about the second gentleman as about the first, but I guessed he was Jewish and was reassured. But only briefly. For now he made me turn around to better examine me.

"First lesson," he said. "We must do something about your *payoth.*"

"No," I shouted with growing fear.

Nothing on earth could have made me give up the two side-curls which made my face look more Jewish.

"We must," he repeated. "With those curls in your eyes, you won't be able to play."

"I don't want to play," I shouted. "Not if you have to cut my *payoth* . . ."

In my childish imagination I had visions of being forced to choose between my musical future and my Jewish faith, and I could hear myself accepting martyrdom.

"Don't be silly," the captain said. "Nobody will cut them off. Who needs them? You want your earlocks, keep them. However, before coming here, you'll have to push them behind your ears. You can put them back in place when you go home. What do you say? Do you agree?"

"No," I replied, trembling. "I am a Jew. A Jew has no right to wear disguises. A Jew who hides his *payoth* is a liar and a fake and should be ashamed of himself."

He stared at me and shrugged his shoulders. "You're stubborn, my little Jewish friend. Just like the rest of your people. Still, I think I'm going to like you anyway. I think you and I will get along."

He was short and heavy-set. His strong features, low forehead and somber, heavy-lidded eyes were impressive. I was afraid to meet his gaze.

"Well," he said. "Hand me that, let me show you what playing means."

He seized the violin and began to play what turned out to be his favorite *doina*. Eyes closed as in a trance, he seemed to plunge back into his childhood, far away, among the gypsies. I was afraid to breathe, but I followed him and watched him make his memories dance. The experience left me wide-eyed and enchanted as never before.

"See?" he said, surprised at finding me still there. "That's the way you'll have to play."

Then he showed me how to stand, how to hold the instrument in my left hand and the bow in my right, how to keep time and make of the violin an extension of my arm, an expression of my soul.

75

While I was practicing, he uncorked the bottle, lifted it to his lips and took several swallows. I shall never know whether he was as satisfied with his pupil as he evidently was with his *cuika*.

Two days later I came back, carrying the same violin and another bottle. From then on, it became a ritual. While he drank, I familiarized myself with the instrument and its sounds. Had he been as good a teacher as he was a drinker, I would perhaps be more than the amateur violinist I am today.

I can see him still: daydreaming, his elbows on the table, the bottle in front of him. He drank without opening his eyes. Sometimes a mysterious anger seized him and he would snatch the violin out of my hands and feverishly perform one of his savage tunes. Appeased, he would order me to play the piece again while he took another swallow from the bottle. As long as there was any *cuika* left, I could practice. The moment the bottle was empty, I had to leave; the lesson was over. Fortunately, his influence on me was limited to music.

Incidentally, I must admit he was a good instructor; I realize it now. In turn severe and forgiving, attentive and absent-minded, patient and intolerant; his mood changed according to the need. In initiating me into the secrets of his art, he communicated its rhythm and fire. And with the years the projected concert at the Borsher Rebbe's became a possibility.

Naturally it never came to pass. My little town was annexed by Hungary, and my Rumanian police captain was transferred before I was quite ready to perform in public.

Father tried hard to find someone to replace him. Five or six potential successors were approached; none appealed to me. In the meantime I had become involved in other studies and other passions. Mute in its case, the violin was relegated to the rank of object, to the sharp displeasure of my parents. Father was to remind me reproachfully of this not long thereafter.

We had just arrived at the camp. Both of us were immediately assigned to the orchestra commando. Being a novice, my father naïvely believed that professional musicians had a better chance for survival. And so he told me: "See? If you had listened to me, if you had not given up the violin, you would not only be in the commando, you would now be a full-fledged member of the orchestra."

It was as if he were scolding me for having missed an important career elsewhere, on the other side, among the rich and powerful.

In truth, I was glad then not to possess the mastery required for admission to the orchestra. I could not have played, not there. Or: I could have played, which would have been worse.

Besides, my father was wrong: the musicians in our commando, so envied by us, did not survive.

FIRST ROYALTIES

I F S O M E O N E had told me when I was a child that one day I would become a novelist, I would have turned away, convinced he was confusing me with someone else.

For the pattern of my future had then seemed clear. I would pursue my studies in the same surroundings with the same zeal, probing the sacred texts and opening the gates to the secret knowledge that permits fulfillment by transcending self.

Novels I thought childish, reading them a waste of time. You had to be a fool to love the fictitious universe made of words when there was the other, immense and boundless, made of truth and presence. I preferred God to His creation, silence to revelation.

As for France—whose language I chose for my tales—its name evoked visions of a mythical country, real only because mentioned in Rashi and other commentaries on the Bible and Talmud.

It took a war—and what a war—to make me change my road, if not my destiny.

The story of that change might not have been mine. And I might not have written it.

My first royalties were two bowls of soup, awarded me for a creative work never set to paper. The taste of that soup still lingers in my mouth.

. . . It happened a long time ago, in a place where all persons wore the same mask beneath the same face, and all faces had the same blank stare.

I was young, barely out of yeshiva, too young to have become accustomed to the tephillin's leather straps. My left arm still bore their imprint. In my imagination, I was still running after my teachers; I was their disciple, though not their heir. While carrying on my shoulders stones heavier than my body, I saw myself surrounded by flickering candles, pondering questions formulated centuries earlier in other places, on the other side of the world and perhaps even of history.

In the beginning, I had enough strength left to resist. Also it was my luck—yes, luck—to work next to a former Rosh-Yeshiva from Galicia. I don't remember his name; perhaps I never knew it. As for his face, I never really looked at it. Only his voice has stayed with me, unforgotten and unforgettable, deep and sepulchral, the voice of a friend, a sick friend.

"You are new here? Instead of welcoming you, let me tell you your first duty: you must hold on. Do you hear? Hold on at any cost. You must not allow yourself to be tainted by evil, yours or anyone else's."

Bent over, without looking at me, he continued in a voice weaker but gentler than before: "Think of your soul and you'll resist better. The soul is important and the enemy knows it; that's why he tries to corrupt it before destroying us. Do not let him. The soul counts for more than the body. If your soul maintains its strength, your body too will withstand the test. I tell you this because you have just arrived; you are still capable of listening. In a month it will be too late. In a month you will no longer know what having a soul could possibly mean."

"Isn't the soul supposed to be immortal?" I asked innocently.

We were digging. He stopped, lowered his voice, as if unwilling to hear his own words, and replied: "You will soon learn that this is neither the place nor the time to speak of immortality."

Afraid lest I had offended him, I was about to apologize, but he was quick to resume: "To hold on, little brother, take my advice: protect your soul and it will protect you. You have the means. It's simple: all you have to do is study."

"Study what?"

"Torah, naturally. What else is there to study? It is the only road leading anywhere. Take it and follow it. As before, better than before, with even greater zeal than when you were at home."

"That's insane," I said in disbelief. "How do you expect me to study here? Without teachers or books?"

"You'll soon learn to get along without them. You'll leap two thousand years back into the past. Here too the Talmud will serve as refuge. You'll study it the way it was taught long ago in Sura and Pumbedita: from memory. In this place, little brother, we have no choice. Whether we want it or not, each one of us owes it to himself to be, all at once, Rabbi Yohanan ben Zakkai, Rabbi Akiba, Rabbi Yehuda . . ."

The sudden appearance of a *kapo* made him stop. The danger past, he continued with renewed vigor: ". . . and this means that all the rabbis, all the sages, all the saints, from the very beginning of our history, have been preparing for this place. This is our new yeshiva, the new dwelling of Torah and the Shekhinah."

He became my teacher.

"Where were you in your studies—before?" he wanted to know.

I told him: the tractate on Shabbat, third chapter.

"What page?"

I told him.

"Good. Let's continue. We have no time to lose."

He knew the entire tractate by heart. Better yet: the whole Talmud. The one from Jerusalem and the Babylonian. And all the Commentaries. He had undoubtedly been an *ilui* in his hometown, respected and admired for his erudition and wisdom. Here, like all of us, he was ravaged by hunger, lost in anonymity. But to him, this was unimportant. What mattered was to be able, thanks to a single disciple, to become Rosh-Yeshiva again, even here, in the camp. Since I was ready to receive, he knew he could give. And as long as he went on giving, he was as strong as life, even stronger perhaps. To me, he became the personification of the Jew's characteristic need to transmit his legacy; and he knew that he was timeless and indestructible.

In the weeks that followed, we studied together many hours, sometimes without interruption, losing our awareness of what surrounded us.

Our system? First he would quote a passage, then I would repeat it. Later we discussed its every aspect. In this way I learned more with him than I had learned in all my years of study at home.

Came the day of separation. Unexpected and irrevocable, like everything else at camp. The Rosh-Yeshiva did not have time to give me his blessing; he was transferred to another camp and I never heard from him again.

His departure forced me to interrupt my studies for the second time. Besides, even if my teacher had stayed, I could not have continued. My strength was deserting me. In the end, resolution gave way and followed the body: weakened one like the other, one by the other.

A miserable crust of moldy bread came to contain more truth, more eternity than all the pages of all the books put together. Reduced to the level of matter, spirit became matter. Just as our bodies came to look alike, so our hearts harbored one single wish: bread and soup, thicker, if possible, than yesterday's. We were hungry for nothing else.

One evening our block leader, a Czech Jew more humane than his colleagues, announced his decision to offer two bowls of soup as a reward for the best story. The unscheduled literary contest was open to all and attracted a large number of contestants; the inmates all wanted to be heard. The block leader presided, pointing to one man after another: each storyteller stepped forward and had three minutes to demonstrate his talent. One told of past glory, another of present anguish. Some spoke with humor, others with emotion. Some used grandiloquent phrases, others pleaded in soft whispers: all hoped for our pity.

My turn came almost at the end. In fact, not having offered to participate, I was taken by surprise. The block leader's attention had probably been caught by my youth; no doubt he wanted to show his compassion by giving me a chance.

"And you, young man, what do you have to tell us?"

"Me? Nothing."

"How come? Aren't you hungry?"

"No, sir," I answered without hesitation.

"Liar!"

I was watching him, and myself, from a distance. I didn't reply.

He raised his voice: "Imbecile! I'm offering you a chance and you refuse? Aren't you interested in staying alive?"

"You don't understand, sir. I have nothing to tell . . . and everything I need; thank you anyway."

"You *are* crazy!"

"No, sir. I am sane. And I have what I want. Thank you very much."

Taken aback, irritated, he began questioning me. Who was I, where was I from, how long had I been here, and why could I not invent a story capable of filling my stomach.

"Because my stomach is already full," I answered with conviction. "It's true, sir. I don't want anything. Neither your soup nor your pity. If you really must know, I have just eaten. As much as I cared to. Believe me. I have eaten more and better than you."

"More and better . . . than I?" he said, looking annoyed. "You? Today? Here? You are positively mad, you must be. Mad. Done for. You'll die. And I thought I could help you . . ."

He studied me with such painful disbelief that I decided to take him into my confidence. And I began describing, in detail, the sumptuous meal which, in my imagination, I had just savored. The dishes, the wines, the fruits, the dessert.

By inviting him to the feast, I reminded him that it was Friday night. The Shabbat meal. White tablecloth, silver candlesticks. The serenity, the joy. My mother, her hands shielding her face, blesses the candles. My little sister is setting the table. Take care, little sister, we have guests. She rearranges the settings. The door opens and there is my grandfather, preceded by the ritual song inviting the angels of Shabbat to honor us with their presence. Father blesses the wine, breaks the bread. The maid serves the fish. Grandfather eats with appetite and sings with enthusiasm. When his son-in-law tries to start a discussion on politics, he interrupts: No, no, not tonight, no politics during the Shabbat meal. Because, you see, it is Shabbat in our home and in God's: peace and joy of Shabbat to all who need it, everywhere.

I used simple words: it was the child in me speaking, sharing his dream. Surrounding me, in a large circle, the inmates listened, shaking their heads. For each of them I became the child he once had been. The block leader himself seemed far away.

"It takes a long time, the Friday night meal," I said. "Because of the *zemiroth*, the songs. There are so many. We love them all. For the fervor, the nostalgia they contain, man is privileged to express them. So, why hurry? We have time, plenty of time. The worker will not go to work tomorrow, the traveler will not travel, the vagabond, resting at last, will not dread the hour of waking.

It is Shabbat, and the soul needs but another soul to sanction and perfect creation. The body needs nothing. Not this evening, not after such a Shabbat meal . . ."

There was silence in the barracks long after I had finished my tale. The block leader was the first to shatter the mood by shouting: "Bravo, young man! Bravo! Well done!" And turning toward the men: "I nominate him as the winner. Any objections?"

The question was rhetorical, of course. He did not need their approval; nor would anyone have dared to disagree.

So, with great ceremony, he handed me the two bowls of thick soup. Followed by envious eyes, I took my prizes and carried them to my bunk. There I hid one bowl and plunged my spoon into the other. Then I stirred and stirred a long, long time before allowing myself a taste.

And nausea welled up inside me, uncontrollable, overwhelming. I had the oppressive feeling that it was my story itself I was swallowing—a story impoverished and diminished for having been told; its source a memory grown dim and less and less my own.

DIALOGUES III

Is it me *you're watching with such hostility?*
Yes. You.

Do you know me?
I used to know you.

Have we met before?
Often. Too often.

Where?
Over there.

Really? I don't remember seeing you.
But I remember you.

What did I look like?
Black.

What???
You were black, all over. The truncheon, the smoke, the killers' evil eyes, the victims' lifeless eyes: black, all black. The barbed wire, the watchtowers, the stones, the bloodless lips: everything that was black —was you . . .

It's my favorite color.

... I could see nothing but you. From morning till night and until the next dawn. You, you, only you and always you. The stranger whose hot, gasping breath I felt behind me during roll call, the sick man full of envy for the crust of bread I meant to save for later: you. The friend clinging to me and the dying man clinging to my friend, the brute hoarding in his tin dish a soup thicker than mine, the father stumbling and the son too terrified to help him, the *kapo* meting out punishment and the prisoners submitting in silence or with screams: it was you, you, always you.

Strange: I don't remember your face.
You were busy, overworked. We were many.

Still ... I have a good memory ... I don't usually forget ... Are you sure ...
Sure, I'm sure. I was there! Your prey, your object! Covered by your black shadow! I was your thing ... your power was unmatched, unmatchable. You were the absolute. You suggested infinity. We ran from you toward you. To escape was impossible: we were inside you.

Why are you so excited? You yell and yell. Are you angry with me? Now?
I was angry with you.

But why? Since I let you get away.
... You shouldn't have.

That's what you call gratitude. If I'd known ...
Go on: If you'd known?

Nothing.
If you'd known, you would not have spared me. Is
    that it?

Perhaps.
Why did you spare me?

Because I didn't know—I just finished telling you.
You're trying to avoid the issue—why?

All right. Let's say you were too young.
There were others younger than I. You took them.

Let's say you were more deserving.
Deserving? I? You're lying. I was no better than my
    comrades and certainly no better than the last
    friends I had.

Perhaps someone interceded in your behalf.
And who might that have been?

Your ancestors. Or your teachers. How should I know?
Then it was not just pure chance? You knew what you
    were doing? You were more than an intermediary?
    More than an instrument?

Much more.
And your decisions were deliberate and not arbitrary?
    You knew why—and to what purpose—you sent
    some straight into the abyss and others on a tortuous
    road obscured by illusions? You had a well-defined
    plan, a program, a goal?

Would you like me to say yes?
Of course. But I want the truth.

88

*Too bad. Because the answer is no. I followed no guide-
lines, proceeded according to no principle. Nobody
told me the nature of my task. Nobody instructed
me not to cross certain limits, not to touch certain
lives. My deeds were part of no pattern and bore
no significance. I did my work in an almost absent-
minded way, without getting involved. And yet,
ordinarily, I am meticulous. I never make mistakes.
I study the terrain—so to speak—before making an
appearance. It's underhanded, I know, but my job
demands it. To me, every being is an individual
case. To be gauged and probed. So as to avoid
errors and confusion. What happens to a man bearing my seal can happen only to him. But over there
it was different. One could take the place of another.*

The dead could have not died?

Of course.

And the others could have not survived?

Naturally.

You're not saying this to deceive me or hurt me? You
really were not carrying out anyone's will? Not
implementing any law in accordance with definite
criteria? You were not acting a part? Not playing
a game?

I was indifferent. Absent-minded. Better still: I was free.

What about your name? After all, it does show your
subservient status! You're expected to carry out
missions assigned by your master—our master!
He's the one who tells you where to go and whom
to seize—isn't he?

*As a rule, yes. Only there, I was in charge: I was
    sovereign. I did what I pleased. He never inter-
    fered, never intervened. Like him, I had no name,
    or too many. All names were mine. He was amused,
    but I was bored.*
Then it was . . . pure chance?

Pure chance.
I could just as easily have gone the other way?

Exactly.
That's horrible.

What did you say?
It's more horrible, more odious than I thought.

What?
So it was pure chance, pure chance, pure chance.

*

*If it means so much to you, you could come with me
    now, you know. It's never too late.*
It's not the same any more.

Did I change so much?
You didn't.

But you did?
No. I didn't either.

Then what has changed?
The relationship between us. Before, it was you and I.
    Now, we are no longer alone. If I follow you,
    others will be affected.

Don't tell me you're happy!
That's not it.

You think you're useful, indispensable?
That's not it either.

Then what is it?
Before, I was you. In the eyes of the man standing be-
    hind me in the breadline and in the eyes of the old
    man whose chances for survival crumbled away
    hour after hour: my youth, my resistance were
    what condemned him. They saw you in me. That
    is over. I am weaker, infinitely weaker than you,
    but I am no longer you.

Are you serious?
More than ever.

Then I pity you.
You know that word?

*Yes, I know that word, I know all words! I pity you be-
    cause you are getting weak. You accept only what
    suits you. Know this: whether you follow me or
    not, for certain people I shall remain you. It is of
    little importance whether you believe me or not;
    they do. And that's enough for me. As far as
    they're concerned, it is beyond the realm of chance.*
You should not have spared me over there, you shouldn't
    have.

*

Come closer. Whom do you wish to see?
You know.

*Look carefully, you will see them. Will you recognize
    them?*
I think so.

Can you see them yet?
Not yet.

Come a little closer.
I can see them now.

All of them?
Not all.

Who is missing?
A child.

He must be there. Look again.
I don't see him.

That's probably your fault, not his. But the others, can you see them?
Clearly. They've hardly changed. Only they seem to be suffering from the cold. To warm themselves, they press against each other. They're trembling.

Are they afraid?
They're beyond fear.

Why are they trembling?
I don't know.

Ask them.
I don't dare.

You're not going to speak to them?
I am speaking to them. They don't seem to hear. And yet, they're looking at me; they see me but they won't speak.

That too is probably your fault, not theirs.
Probably, yes.

Say, now you're the one that's trembling!
I wasn't aware of it. I thought that I too was beyond
   fear.

Then it must be anger.
I hope so.

*Now, just a minute! You better watch yourself! Control
   your nerves! And above all, do me a favor: don't
   touch the mirror; it might break. And I cannot do
   without it; I need it, do you hear me, I need it!*
More than I?

*More than all of you. For you, it's a chance to dream,
   for me it's an incitement to action.*
Don't worry. I won't be the one to break your mirror:
   the child will. And you are powerless against him.
   Eyes have no hold over him. And he's not trembling. He is dead. You permitted him to escape
   your grasp.

*It's incredible: you refuse to understand. I wasn't the
   one who killed him. It was you.*

WAITING

I WOULD LIKE to tell you the story
of the woman named Barbara, only I don't know it. She
refused to tell it to me. Less afraid to be judged than to be
remembered, she attempted by every possible means to
exorcise the story from people's memories, to the point
of almost losing her own. She would say: "Men, those
fools, think they're buying my body: what I'm selling is
my memory."

Her past, like everyone else's, was made of words, and
her future of images. Like everyone else, she had a story
she did not like, a story shared with countless strangers
whose sullen faces and vulgar peculiarities followed one
another endlessly, as in a play of mirrors where the same
eerie silhouette reflects itself into infinity. She took pleasure
in mutilating and disguising it; she dragged it through
the mud only to adorn it later with pretty lies: her tale was
false from beginning to end. But wasn't this distortion
her only chance to alter it beyond recognition even to
herself?

No matter. Now that she has discarded her memory,
she will somehow acquire a story that will be hers and
hers alone, an unblemished story beginning and ending
with herself, a story lived by no one else and still

unknown even to God. A story that men, those fools, will never understand.

I was still very young. So young that I would instinctively quicken my step when in my wanderings I happened to pass through those dimly lit, airless side streets, where restless nocturnal creatures hugged the walls, seeming forever to expect a friend or enemy, never the same, their bodies poised against the inevitable stab in the back.

I stepped out of their way, I avoided them. They filled me with an obscure fear. Each time one of them accosted me, whispering and gazing lewdly into my eyes, I lowered my head and blushed. I stammered: "No, thank you," conscious of the sin I was committing, for it was "Yes, thank you" that I should have said.

In the Bible, *kedosha* means "holy," while *kedesha* means "prostitute." That the two words should have one root was to me a disturbing mystery. But I usually lacked both the courage and the money to resolve it. I resisted temptation but it did not make me proud.

That summer night, however, things were different. Unable to fall asleep, I had gone out for a walk along the Seine. I was gloomy. For weeks I had been feeling anxious and aloof, sinking into paralyzing sadness. Books bored and irritated me and so did my friends. Since I had nothing to do, I spent my days idly prowling through the city, in the grip of a solitude whose origin escaped me. Something had crept between life and myself; I saw it slipping away and did not lift a finger to hold it back: let it go. I felt untouched even in the deepest abyss. Absurdity prevailed.

After a long walk I emerged on a small square, Rue Saint-

Denis, near Les Halles, the central market. It must have been past midnight. A hot wind was blowing through the trees. Four women were at their separate posts. From time to time they came together to exchange jokes or advice, then dispersed again, alert and on the lookout. To attract customers, they used a highly efficient strategy: they operated like a night patrol at the front seeking to establish contact with the enemy.

A man appeared, walked up to one of them and after a brief discussion, shook his head and turned away. Seconds later he had disappeared around the corner, the last customer. Night was deepening, the city was asleep. "What a life!" sighed one of the four.

It took them more than an hour to notice the young student's presence. Moving in from four directions at once, they quickly formed a circle around him.

"How about it, honey?" a redhead asked.

I stared at her a long time before hearing myself reply: "No, not tonight."

"Why not?" her short, plump companion wanted to know.

"I wish to remain here."

"Oh, I see, the rascal prefers looking," said the third.

They burst out laughing; I didn't react. Their laughter was obscene. Their gaping mouths were like those cracks that appear and surreptitiously widen in the dilapidated walls abounding in that section of Paris. Run away? Not now. Their teasing meant nothing: I wasn't really here, I was nowhere.

"You're expecting somebody, maybe?" snickered the redhead.

"Yes. Somebody."

"She's letting you wait and that's not very nice."

"He is not nice," I said. "And he likes to keep people waiting. Besides, I enjoy waiting for him."

"We could keep you company," suggested the red-head, speaking for the group. "That's our job. We'll make you a special deal."

"No, thanks. I wait better when I'm alone."

"He might be pleased to find us here with you, don't you think?"

"No."

"Say, are you speaking for yourself or for him?"

"For both of us. I know he likes solitude. And silence."

"Then tell us his name. Perhaps we know him; you'd be surprised how many people we know. Isn't that right, girls? Tell us what he looks like, if he is rich, if he's fun, and something about his vices and habits. He might turn out to be an interesting customer."

I shrugged my shoulders and didn't answer. I wasn't in the mood to play this senseless game.

"My God," the redhead continued, "he certainly is rude! Here we are worrying about his well-being and he doesn't even answer! You could at least tell us who you're waiting for? We promise not to bite."

"Somebody," I said, barely opening my mouth.

They were sneering. I stared back defiantly. Any other time I would have sought a place to hide, to cleanse and chastise myself. Not now. I felt calm, indifferent: it was not me they were trying to provoke.

Suddenly the fourth girl, the one who had not spoken yet, leaned toward me. "And if I were to tell you that I am the one you're waiting for?" she whispered so softly the others could not hear.

Her hair hung down her partly bared back. She was eying me coldly, thoughtfully. I could smell her breath, heavy with alcohol. Now it was my turn to burst out laughing. The one I had been seeking for so many years: a woman! A shameless woman who chose to sell rather than give herself, a woman for whom to be and to have were one, a woman intimate with men she despised. And to think that in my childhood I had imagined meeting this being on the crests of mountains and in the depths of contemplation. The women were staring at me in amazement. I was laughing, but neither my laughter nor my voice were my own.

"Well?" murmured the girl with the long hair.

"Come, Barbara, forget it," the others said, pulling her by the arm. For them, the show was over.

"Leave me alone," Barbara snapped.

"You must be crazy! Don't you see the poor child is broke?"

"Leave me alone."

"You've had too much to drink! That's it!"

They moved away, their comments lost in the night.

"Your friends are right," I said after a pause. "I am penniless."

"I don't give a damn," she answered, her voice icy. "I like you."

She stroked my cheek and added in a tone intended to be gentle and affectionate: "I like you and that's what counts. Let's forget everything else. Come with me."

"Where to?"

"My place. I live close by. We'll be more comfortable. Come."

"No, thank you."

"Are you afraid? Shy? Would you rather we go to your place?"

"I'm not afraid and I don't want to go anywhere."

She looked at me hard, wrinkling her brow. "You're Jewish, aren't you?"

"Yes, I am," I said, not at all surprised. "How did you guess?"

"Your accent, your voice, the way you say no."

"I'm Jewish, and that means I'm not afraid. Fear no longer is my concern."

She sat down beside me without taking her eyes off mine. In the dark, her grossly painted face was terrifying, revealing all the humiliations of her body and soul.

"Do you enjoy making love?" she asked coolly.

"That depends."

"What about me? Would you like to make love to me?"

"I don't know."

"Would you try it to find out?"

"No, thank you."

"Why not?"

I remained silent: it was not me she was questioning, so it was not up to me to answer. She took my hand; I pulled it back.

"Do I disgust you? Is that it?"

"No, not at all. I'm just too warm."

"So am I. And sometimes I disgust myself."

I wanted to say something to soothe her, but my mind was blank. "Let's talk," I said.

99

"What about?"

"You."

She asked me to use the familiar *tu*. "All men do," she explained. It was the first time anyone had categorized me as man.

"All right," I agreed. "But let's talk about you."

"What do you want me to say?" There was a hint of anger in her voice. "I don't like to talk about myself. While taking off their clothes, men always want to know who I am. It's important for them to know on whom they have the honor and pleasure of spitting. I don't answer. Anyway, not truthfully. As it is, my truth is soiled enough. And so I invent, I embroider. I have lots of imagination. You understand?"

"I understand."

I really didn't, I just didn't want to hurt her. I wasn't even listening. It was too hot. I took out my handkerchief and mopped my face. She did the same.

"Am I boring you?" she asked.

"Not at all."

"If I am, say so."

"Not at all. It's the heat."

"Where was I?"

"You were telling me about truth."

"Oh, yes, what was I saying? Men want to know everything, absolutely everything. So I humor them; I make up stories; each one made to order: they would break your heart. Those imbeciles adore stories and confessions. In every man there is a priest who sees in every woman an unhappy whore, a soul to save and console and bring back to the fold. Which offers him the luxury of behaving magnanimously, like a self-appointed or God-appointed protector of widows and orphans. That is what they all come for: not to make love—that too, of course—but to bring us their cheap pity and affection. 'Ah, my little one, you suffered so much as a child, here is another hundred francs. It's a present. You see: I am generous. But in exchange, pretty child, you'll be nice with me, promise?' So I pocket my tip and say thanks very much, mister, thanks very much, Father, you're so good, and kind, and have a heart of gold, the soul of a saint, come here, stretch out on me, I give myself to you, I'll let you do as you please, draw as much pleasure out of me as you wish, as you can, I'm a pleasure machine, don't worry, there'll be enough for everybody, for all the priests and saints still to come. That's what I tell them—joking, crying or beating them, depending on their taste: some like my tears, others are excited only by my fury. See? I'm not worth more than a hundred francs."

She interrupted herself, moistened her lips and said: "And you? What do you want?"

"I have no idea."

"What do you want from me?"

"Nothing, I suppose."

"Do you want me to speak of truth? Like the others?"

"If you wish. But I must warn you again, I haven't a cent."

Once again she seized my hand violently, and this time I let her. At her touch and for the first time that night, I could not keep from trembling. I had just rediscovered my body.

"I like you," she continued, releasing my hand. "I like

you because you're young and poor; because you're Jewish and unafraid. And also because I don't understand you."

She drew back slightly as if to see me better. "I know what you're thinking. That I'm drunk."

"Wrong. I'm not thinking anything."

"Don't interrupt. Please. You're not thinking of anything but you think I'm drunk. One does not exclude the other. Well, it's true. I did drink. Not much. Just a little: with three well-paying customers. I suggested they invite my friends to share the fun; but they didn't go for the idea. You'll manage by yourself, like a big girl, they said. We drank. We did other things. They were pleased and told me so. They left. I kept one bottle. I didn't touch it, I swear, that is, not really. I don't enjoy drinking, not alone, not like that. My head spins when I drink alone. It's spinning now. Feel it: it's spinning, can you tell?"

She began turning her head with such frenzy that I became dizzy. I said: "Yes, indeed, it is spinning."

"You see? I know what I'm saying. I may seem incoherent, but I know what I want to say. If you don't understand, it's because you're Jewish: you're a good listener, but you don't understand."

Her hand moved to her mouth as if to apologize for her blunder. "Did I offend you? No? Good. Still, I do apologize. You must forgive me. You do understand, I know that. I take it all back: you're a Jew, therefore you understand. It's I who don't understand you. See, when I saw you, sitting on your bench, sitting on the night—yes, don't look at me like that, on the night: I say, one can sit on it and lie down on it, one can even dwell in it—when I noticed you there, I immediately knew that you were

someone who understands, someone I cannot understand.
You like hearing me say that, don't you? You're young
and the young love to be told that. Well, I'm going to
make you happy and solemnly declare: I do not understand you. There now, are you glad? Besides, it makes me
glad too. I would so like never to understand. It rarely
happens. Most of the time I understand only too well
and too fast. What do you expect? That's what I'm paid
for. Men, I know them, I can see through their schemes
and pretenses. Immediately. I think to myself: 'Go ahead,
old boy, do your little act, I know before you and better
than you what you're after.' Ha, they think they possess
me when they take my body and fill me with their disgust;
in fact, I'm infallible; I see through them and I spit on
them."

Barbara was telling me her life, and I thought of mine,
and of all human existence, which one single gesture, one
single event can distort, uplift or debase forever. One word
said or said poorly, or not said at all, a train missed, a hand
taken or rejected, and life is no longer what it might have
been. Freedom? A farce. The future is but the product
of the past, which remains beyond our reach; we may no
longer touch it, for it becomes a divinity created by us
and against us. What is done is done, we cannot retrace
our steps, we cannot choose ourselves again. Thus a yes
or a no, every yes and every no, commits man beyond
the present. That is the misunderstanding, the fundamental
injustice of human condition: we accept and refuse situations which will emerge only later, when it is already too
late.

Barbara kept quiet a long time. I should have said something.

She misinterpreted my silence: "You're not exactly talkative. Did you at least listen?"

"Jews are good listeners," I reminded her.

"I also like to listen."

"I have nothing to say."

"Nothing? No reaction? No comment? I have just told you the idiotic story I call my life, and you have nothing to say?"

"Nothing."

"All right. As you wish. But I have a favor to ask of you."

"What sort of favor?"

"Forget what I told you. Immediately. I too want to forget. Promise?"

"Of course. I promise."

She tried to kiss me; I gently pushed her away. "It's frightfully hot," I said.

She took her handkerchief and wiped my face. "Why don't you talk to me? Are you afraid I won't understand? Is that it? But that is precisely what I wish! Tell me anything, so long as I don't understand! Just once in this rotten life I would like not to understand!"

A dense sadness was oppressing me. Barbara brought her face close to mine and I did not pull back. Her lips were on my cheek. I let her. She still smelled of whiskey. I thought: The first woman with whom I speak of love is a streetwalker, a drunken streetwalker who likes Jews because she doesn't understand them. I didn't understand myself.

"You're sad. I know when a man is sad. Come, make love. It's still the best remedy against feeling lonely, believe me, I know. Do you have any idea why sadness was given to man? So that women like me wouldn't die of hunger."

I saw myself with the eyes of my childhood and thought: You will not get away, not this time.

"Well? Are you coming? You won't have to speak or listen. You'll be free."

I got up abruptly. "No, thank you, I don't feel like it."

It was false and true at the same time. I wanted her and was afraid that she might be aware of it.

"You really don't want to? You don't know what you're missing."

A grayish light was slowly tearing the sky. The city was fighting its last battle against a flight of ravens—or were they vultures?—pushing it beyond the horizon. Soon it would be day.

I looked at the woman and held out my hand. "I must leave," I said, hiding my agitation. "Take care."

She hesitated but took my hand and held it tightly. "Goodbye, my little Jew. Where are you going now? Back to your woman, your girl friend?"

"I don't have one."

"Your parents?"

"Perhaps."

A few seconds went by. I added: "They're dead."

A smile flickered across her face. "Well, I certainly don't understand you. Thank you for that."

We each went our separate ways; my head was lowered, she held hers high. I had walked only a few steps when I heard her call a last message: "I forgot something important: I can never have a child! Can you hear me? Never! Never! That is as important as the rest of my story!"

"Your story? What story?"

I shrugged my shoulders and went on my way through the morning mist. A drunken whore, that's what she was, Barbara. Barbara? Was that even her name? Probably not. Marie, Suzanne, Elizabeth, Blanche, Emma, Marcelle. But not Barbara. She took that name so she could tell herself: "It's not me walking the streets; it's Barbara." Who then had I spoken to?

In the following months I was careful to avoid that neighborhood. Then, one night, I felt a desire to see Barbara again. From a bench in the small square near Les Halles, I watched the street, waiting for her to appear. She was gone; night, or perhaps her own never-to-be-told story, had recaptured her.

Another girl had taken her place. She came over to me and asked: "You are looking for somebody?"

"Yes," I said. "Somebody."

"But who?"

I waited before repeating: "Somebody." I added: "A prophet."

"My poor, poor boy. You just go right on looking; but I bet he's up there. And he's busy. Busy making love!"

THE END OF
A REVOLUTIONARY

So mewhere, far away: noisy
streets, crowded with people strolling and laughing, with
window-shoppers and policemen. And much ado. About
nothing. Aimless shouting and calling. And quarreling.
Just for the fun of it.

And I was going to get some rest here, the stranger
thought, more amused than bitter.

He was sitting on the terrace of a sidewalk café, shielded
from the sun, idly watching the passing cars and the
pedestrians dodging them: Even so, I was right to come,
nothing here concerns me.

Three days earlier he was still at home. In his house,
with a woman both gentle and melancholy. And colleagues, some friendly, some envious. Smiles, flatteries and
half-truths. Always the same questions, the same answers.
The same burdens and the same alibis. Suddenly he felt
like leaving it all. Without a word. Leave. For a few days.
Or a few years. And breathe. And remain silent; remain
silent at last. He jumped into a taxi. To the airport. The
first plane out. Anywhere. Don't look at me that way.
Please. Yes, I'll pay. Cash. Anywhere, I said. Hurry.

I was right to come, he thought. Here too I am a
stranger. But it's not the same.

2

The hours flew by. He wasn't aware of time. Before, it had filled him with anguish. Time-conscious? More than that: time-obsessed. Not any more. He was living outside time. No clock, no obligations. No need to pretend being busy, entertained, interested, moved. He would get up and go to sleep whenever he chose. No one would ask: Where were you? Or: Whom did you see? Or: Why are you late? No one would try to make him forget or remember. He would be alone at dusk and still alone at dawn. Not like a prisoner in his cell; like a fugitive in the forest.

His home? He would forget it. His work? To hell with his work. And the woman? So as not to think about her, he began studying the faces around him. A pair of young lovers, isolated from the outside world. What seemed like a gang of thieves plotting. A baffled-looking man sporting a mustache. A woman. Why is she so worried? Let's stop, and look again. Still young, in her twenties, perhaps older. Black hair, fiery eyes, sensual, obstinate lips. Probably waiting for someone, her husband, her lover perhaps. She seems impatient, preoccupied: yes, worried. She has consulted her wristwatch at least ten times. She starts to get up, only to sit down again. The stranger tries to catch her eye. In vain. He smiles at her; she does not respond. He leans toward her and asks her the time; she pretends not to hear.

I don't feel rebuffed. It's her privilege after all. She owes me nothing. Anyway, she distracts me from my thoughts. Isn't that enough?

3

Now she was staring at him. Openly. Without false modesty. She smiled, and now she spoke: "You are not from around here, are you?"

"No. But you are."

"Wrong."

"Are you expecting someone? Someone special?"

"Of course. You."

"Sorry I kept you waiting."

She laughed in a strange way: her face was not smiling, neither were her eyes. Only her voice was gay.

"Please forgive my lack of manners," he said. "I didn't introduce myself properly."

"Don't bother. I detest names."

"Any reason?"

"Names are irrelevant, irrational and deceptively personal. And harmful at that. Don't they trouble you?"

"Sorry." He smiled, blushing. "It's too hot for philosophical discussions. Later perhaps? Over dinner?"

There was amusement in her eyes. "Philosophy and food don't go together in this town. Thanks, anyway. And now I must leave. I have an appointment. Not with you."

"But with some other nameless person like me?"

"Possibly. No, he's not like you. You have a face; he has only a mask."

They both got up.

"May I go with you?"

"I think it would be best if you didn't."

"He is jealous, is that it?"

She hesitated a moment, then went on: "After all, why not? Do come."

She handed him a small suitcase he found rather heavy.

4

They walked awhile without speaking. They had left the main streets and were following a deserted side street. At the end of it loomed a dark, dismal building.

"What's that down there?" asked the stranger.

"Government offices. Stay away from them." And after a pause: "Our own people avoid them when possible."

"Why?"

"Those inside are executioners or victims: police investigators or political prisoners. Would you want to be either?"

They took three more steps.

The young woman stopped. "We must part now. Where are you staying?"

"Hotel Excelsior."

"Room?"

"483."

"I'll remember it . . . just in case."

"Will I see you again?"

"Perhaps."

He was about to insist.

She cut him short. "Go home," she said, a note of impatience in her voice.

"All right. I'll be expecting you—just in case."

He gave her back her suitcase.

5

He returned to his hotel, went down for a sandwich, circled the main square a few times and went to bed.

A deafening explosion awakened him shortly after midnight. He ran to the window but could see nothing. A moment later there was a burst of gunfire. A machine gun crackled briefly and stopped. Then silence again, heavier than before.

Well, thought the stranger, I'll go back to sleep. Let them shoot each other. It's no concern of mine. Tomorrow I'll find out what happened. There's no hurry. This country is not mine, this incident has nothing to do with me. I know neither those doing the shooting nor those being shot at. I just happen to be here. I might easily have been elsewhere.

With the woman I left back home, for instance. Who would invariably be asking the same senseless questions: "What are you thinking about? Where are you? Why do you shut me out?"

To which he would be answering: "I'm not thinking about anything, really."

And it would have gone on:

"I don't believe you."

"That's the trouble with us: even when you believed in me, you didn't believe me."

"It's your fault. You no longer talk to me."

"What do you want me to tell you?"

"Why you no longer talk to me."

He fell asleep, moaning.

6

The bellboy brought his breakfast. "Did you hear the explosion?" he asked, all excited.

"I did. What was it?"

"A bomb."

"Where?"

"Not far from here. At secret police headquarters. Two floors demolished. The colonel killed, his aide too: shot like mad dogs. Nine wounded. It's the revolution, sir! You understand? Dictatorship, corruption, fear, torture: finished, the old regime. Finished! For good! The revolution has won!"

"Good for you."

"Is that all you have to say?"

"What do you want me to say? I'm a foreigner here. I don't even know who is in power or who would like to be. You want to know something else? I don't even care."

"How can you say these things? How can you be so callous? Last night some men were killed, others became heroes—and it doesn't touch you? Doesn't even interest you?"

"I repeat, young man: what happens in this country is not my business. I don't take sides. You want to play games? Fine, but play without me. Leave me out."

"I can't believe you, sir . . . you can't possibly be as insensitive as you wish to appear . . . No one is . . ."

"Listen, young man. If your revolutions prevent my having breakfast in peace, I'll have to reconsider . . ." The stranger tasted the coffee and made a face. "It's lukewarm! Horrible! I like my coffee scalding hot! Whose

fault is that, young man? The old regime's or the revolution's?"

Disgusted, the bellboy rushed out, decided not to apologize.

7

There was repeated knocking at his door, but it
took the stranger a while to hear it. He was shaving and
his electric razor was noisy. As soon as he unplugged it,
he heard the noise. Opening the door, he found himself
facing two angry men.

"Are you deaf?" they shouted.

"Excuse me, but . . ."

"Later. You'll make your excuses later. Let's go."

"You must be crazy."

"Let's go."

"Who are you?"

"Police."

"What do you want?"

"Please follow us."

"But what have I done?"

"Later. You'll get all the answers later. We have our
orders. Get dressed. Please."

The stranger was rapidly losing his composure. "But I
haven't done anything! I've just arrived! Surely this is a
case of mistaken identity! I'm a foreigner! I demand to see
my consul! I know my rights!"

The two policemen didn't even take the trouble to confer. "Don't get excited and don't make a fuss; it won't do
you any good. These stalling tactics can only hurt your
case."

What was the use of arguing? Trying to look detached,

he picked up his jacket, his billfold and a handkerchief, and declared himself ready to go. His things? He didn't care; he could do without them. It was just like him to divest himself of his possessions. On his travels, he invariably distributed them among strangers, arriving home empty-handed.

Followed by the two policemen, he left the hotel and was pushed into a black unmarked car parked a few steps away, near the corner.

It's a good thing I brought my handkerchief, he thought as he wiped his face. It was going to be a hot day.

8

Yet he was not afraid. He found the adventure disconcerting, incomprehensible—nothing more. What did it all mean? They were going to put him in prison, condemn or perhaps even execute him. By mistake. Everything was possible in these countries. Who do they think I am? he wondered. Well, he'd soon find out.

No, he was not frightened. Simply amused. At last something will happen to me, he thought. Too late? No, it wasn't too late. The last day, the last hour count more than all the others.

Life had recently become tiresome, marginal, not unlike a robot's. He was untouched by surprise or disappointment, joy or sorrow, poverty or love. Resigned to apathy, he let himself drift. His days were all alike, his nights grew longer. His dreams became burdens. Everything had been said and experienced; he had drained the cup. Never again would he know the rapture of creation or the despair of failure. Never again would he delight in the joys of new encounters. Death itself would not be new; let it come.

Here or elsewhere, now or later: he didn't care. For years now he had been dead without knowing it. Now his death would become fact, a part of reality. And absurdity. He should actually welcome it. To die for nothing, out of sheer negligence, in someone else's stead, should actually please him. A death, an end he neither sought nor fled, should suit him. Since his existence had become meaningless, why then should his death have a meaning?

Such were the thoughts running through his mind while he was being driven toward the young woman he had met the afternoon before.

9

The office in which she received him had belonged to the former governor of the city. Three armed guards stood at attention.

"Glad to see you again," said the young woman with a tired smile.

He tried to conceal his astonishment. "So am I. Tell me: did you send the police?"

"Naturally."

"Well, well," he said admiringly. "When you feel like seeing someone again, you know just what to do. My compliments."

"If the policemen were rude, I apologize."

"No apologies necessary. Police are the same everywhere. But you know, if you wanted to see me that badly, you could have chosen some simpler way than starting a revolution, don't you think?"

She didn't flinch. "Revolutions are not started by individuals for individuals, but for the people. Ours is no exception. I am sorry I forgot to tell the police chief that you did your part."

"My part in what?"

"In last night's revolution. You are not a prisoner, you are our honored guest. Better still, our hero."

"I wish you were speaking for yourself—not for your countrymen. Your hero? I'd be delighted. Any time. Theirs? Never."

"Your modesty is to your credit. However, the facts remain: your courage is known. That case you helped me carry yesterday, do you know what it contained? A bomb, a powerful bomb. Meant to destroy the secret police head-quarters. With your help I managed to cross several check points. Thanks to your assistance, the operation was a success. That is why . . ."

She stopped and motioned to one of her assistants, who handed her a small rectangular box. Opening it, she went on: ". . . on behalf of the Revolutionary Movement for National Liberation, I hereby bestow upon you the first medal for revolutionary heroism."

As in a dream he watched himself extend his hand and, a bewildered grin on his face, accept the box. "You're mad," he said. "I don't know your name and you don't know mine."

Her comment was brief: "If that's all that bothers you, I can reassure you. When you leave here, buy a newspaper. You will see that by now the entire country knows both of us."

Then she expressed regret that due to other pressing matters she could not stay with him longer. She saw him to the door and whispered: "Don't be angry. We need a foreign hero. To show our enemies that we have friends abroad."

"Thanks for having thought of me."

"You are angry; I am sorry."

He looked at her and smiled. "Forget it," he said. "I am not angry, not really. Besides, what difference does it make?"

Nothing made any difference.

10

Back at the hotel, he had to face a large crowd of newsmen, both foreign and domestic. They showered him with provocative questions, which he dodged with tact and diplomacy. Several microphones were shoved under his nose and the national hero had to improvise the usual statements which all heroes of all revolutions must improvise in all languages, praising the same leaders and invoking the same principles. All things considered, it was not too difficult a task.

After the press conference, the bellhop came in, blushing like a schoolboy. "I should have known . . . guessed who you were . . . How stupid of me . . . Will you ever forgive me?"

For several days—or was it several weeks?—the hero could not go out without being mobbed by autograph-seekers. Women smiled at him, men greeted him with respect. Yet fame had no effect on him. It did not make him feel better. Or worse. He was carried from one celebration to another, from one political function to another, performing as in a dream.

More than once he almost left the tiny republic to return

to his own country, his hometown. Since he had not succeeded in overcoming his apathy, he might just as well be living at home, surrounded by familiar objects. But each time he postponed his departure. Somehow he knew that this adventure had a sequel, an ending. It was this element of the unknown he loved and sought; he loved nothing else. And sometimes not even that.

11

Then one morning he had a nightmare: there was knocking at the door, they had come to arrest him. Again? Yes, again. Once more he went through the same motions. In the street below, the same unmarked black car was parked near the same corner. It made its way toward the same building. He was led into the same room and found himself face to face with the same woman, aged and ravaged, her hands tied. There was blood seeping from her mouth and emptiness in her eyes.

"You are accused of revolutionary activities against the government and the people," said the officer, tall and serene, in a monotonous voice. "Guilty or not guilty?"

"Not guilty," he replied mechanically.

"Too bad. Your denial makes it worse for you. We have witnesses. Look at this person. You know her, she knows you. And she confessed. You were her accomplice. A traitor's accomplice, that's what you are."

"No," said the stranger. "I am nothing of the kind. I am nothing and nobody."

"Very well," said the officer. "The witness will repeat her testimony."

And the young woman obeyed: "Yes, he was my accomplice; yes, we did collaborate in armed attacks; yes, he knew it was a bomb he was carrying." She stared at him and hissed: "Stop denying the obvious, friend. Why let yourself be tortured? They know everything. The revolution—yours and mine—has failed, and we have to pay the price: it's part of the game, you know. So follow my advice: sign your confession."

In his dream, he was going to shout that she was lying, that she was losing her mind, that he was not guilty— anything but guilty, at least of this crime—but in the face of so much absurdity, he chose not to humiliate himself. So, rather than protest, he began to laugh, gently at first and then with all his might.

Dumbfounded, the officer gaped at him in silence. Then he summoned a guard to take away the young woman. As she was being led past the stranger, she whispered: "I'm sorry, friend, but our movement will need martyrs, innocent martyrs especially."

She went out, and the stranger's eyes followed her. What a strange dream, he thought. What a strange life. One could die laughing.

THE DEATH
OF MY TEACHER

"... M ASTERING thirty ancient and modern languages, knowing by heart the Vedas as well as the Zohar, he felt at home in every culture, in every role. Always dirty, unkempt, he looked like a vagabond turned clown, or a clown turned vagabond. He wore a tiny hat, always the same, on top of his huge round head; his glasses with their thick, always foggy lenses only blurred his vision . . . For three years, in Paris, I was his disciple. And under his guidance I learned a great deal about the dangers of language and reason and about the ecstasies of wisdom and madness. I learned about the mysterious progress of thought through centuries and the equally mysterious persistence of hesitation through centuries of thought; but nothing about the secret which, though consuming him, protected him against a diseased humanity."

That is how, in *Legends of Our Time*, I described without naming him, my master and teacher Rav Mordecai Shushani. If I reveal his name now, it is because he is no longer alive.

I received word of his death from another writer, Jean Halperin, who also considers himself his disciple. The news was given to me without details, because it was thought that

I knew. I did not. I knew Shushani had settled in Montevideo, as mysterious as ever; nothing else.

On one occasion he had invited me to resume our studies together. From time to time I felt—and resisted—the urge to take the first plane leaving for Uruguay, to see him at least one more time, to compare him with the image I had retained. Also I wanted to be roused again; suspended between heaven and earth and permitted to see what brings them together and what sets them apart. But I was afraid. I wrote: ". . . I tremble each time I think of him in Montevideo, where he still awaits me, where he still calls to me; I am afraid to plunge into his legend which condemns us both, me to doubt and him to immortality."

A young man in Montevideo wrote me describing his last hours: sitting on a lawn, surrounded by students, he was teaching them Talmud when suddenly he paused in mid-sentence; a moment later he had stopped breathing. In Jewish tradition, such death is called *mitat neshika:* the angel comes and embraces the chosen one like a friend and takes him along without inflicting pain.

And in his pockets they found my tale about my encounters with him.

So I know that he read it. But I shall never know what he thought of the portrait I had drawn. One thing is certain: he recognized himself.

Others recognized him despite my efforts to disguise the image. His disciples of one year, or one night, took pains to tell me they were not fooled: "The Wandering Jew, in your book, is Rav Shushani, isn't it?"

I myself thought I had exaggerated; yet I had told the truth. Yes, he did visit faraway countries; yes, he did receive unusually high fees for his lectures, fees he then gave to charity; yes, he did behave like one of the hidden Just Men who enter exile and anonymity before offering salvation to their fellow men; yes, he was greater than the legend surrounding his person.

A famous Yiddish novelist told me:

In the early fifties I happened to be in Boston for a lecture. I was going to begin when a small dirty-looking man, wearing a ridiculous hat, pushed me away from the microphone and shouted: "Ladies and gentlemen, your guest tonight has no right to address you, you or any other audience!" In the commotion that followed, the chairman angrily rebuked him: "Are you out of your mind? Who are you, anyway?" "Never mind who I am," answered the heckler. "But I know who he is. A faker, that's who he is. I read an article he once wrote in a Yiddish newspaper in Paris. And he misquoted the Midrash. Anyone who misquotes the sources has no right to speak in public!" I thought he was mentally disturbed, and so did everyone else. True, I had served as editor of a Yiddish daily in postwar Paris. But that was long ago—in the late forties—I published articles five, six times a week. How could I remember? But he, Rav Shushani, remembered and forced me to remember. I had to apologize before being permitted to speak that evening. Several years later I came to Montevideo, also for a lecture. I was about to begin when I noticed a familiar face in the audience. Terror-stricken, I announced that I would not speak unless Rav Shushani left the room. Since the community didn't know him yet, they thought I had gone mad. But despite their efforts to soothe me, I stuck by my decision. That evening, there was no lecture.

Recently, during a weekend in Oslo, I visited a childhood friend, Herman Kahan. We compared our post-war adventures.

He reminisced: "For a time, while waiting for my Norwegian visa, I lived in Paris. I often would visit an unpretentious synagogue where I met . . ."

He was remembering and smiling. So I continued for him: ". . . a mysterious character who possessed all the keys to all the gates and his name was Rav Shushani."

"How did you know?" my friend exclaimed in total bewilderment.

"There is something about all those who ever met him. They can recognize each other. But tell me your story."

"We studied every evening. It went on for weeks. One day he told me his trade: gold merchant. Soon afterwards he disappeared. When next I heard from him he was in Australia. With some of my money."

By the time my friend received Rav Shushani's letter from Australia, Rav Shushani was already in a kibbutz in Israel.

When did I see him last? A year ago, in Paris. As I left my hotel on Boulevard Saint-Germain, I noticed a familiar-looking vagabond; he was engaged in lively discussion with a pretty girl who was trying to sell him one of the new-left publications. It's him, I thought. No, it can't be; he is in Montevideo. The man standing there in front of the hotel only looks like him. Yet the resemblance was so striking that I felt the urge to ask him a direct question: "Aren't you Rav Shushani?" But I didn't want the girl to think I was really interested in her. And so I circled around them again and again until I remembered I had an appointment. Returning to my hotel, I told myself it couldn't possibly have been him.

That same evening, in Strasbourg, Claude Hemmendinger, editor of the *Tribune Juive*, casually remarked: "By the way, did anyone tell you that Rav Shushani has reappeared in Paris?"

So he did see me. And wanted me to see him and miss this last opportunity to speak to him again. He wanted me to go on carrying inside me the same remorse and nostalgia as before.

He was buried in Jerusalem. His admirers and disciples all over the world had been ready to raise funds to take his earthly remains to the Holy City. But there was no need for that. After his death, it was discovered he was rich, richer than many of his followers.

Also discovered among his belongings were several manuscripts, probably containing what might well be his most important ideas and opinions. Except that nobody could decipher them. It was his way of leaving behind still another mystery, a final one.

Having in my possession several letters in his handwriting, I wanted to try my luck with the manuscripts. A few pages were given to me. I read them several times and had to give up: I could read them but could not understand their meaning.

Several months after his death I received a letter from a man claiming to be Shushani's closest living relative: "Since Rav Shushani concerns and haunts you that much, and since he is no longer with us, let me tell you the truth about him."

And he did tell me what he claimed to be the truth about Rav Shushani: his name, his origins, his secret voyages. The mystery was solved.

But the letter contained a postscript: "I am telling you all this because I think you ought to know. However, you are not to disclose the facts to anyone, not now, not ever."

If I choose to obey, it is because I am sure that this is what Rav Shushani himself would have wanted.

Even if all his disciples, everywhere, were to begin speaking about him—and nobody else—we would not know more about who he really was, about what shadows he fled or sought, or the nature of his power and torment.

POSTWAR: 1948

IT WAS A FRIDAY AFTERNOON. Israel had just declared its independence. The world, poised between amazement and anguish, held its breath: Would the Jewish people, in realizing its ancient dream, finally change course and destiny?

I was a stateless student living in Paris, but in my imagination I was a soldier in Jerusalem. Filled with tension and disbelief, I devoured the special editions that succeeded one another hourly. I wanted to be part of the event unfolding far away.

At nightfall I made my way to the synagogue for Shabbat services. Not so much to pray as to enter a dialogue and be part of a community. Prayers had not yet begun. It was getting late, but the excited worshippers were discussing politics and strategy: Could the Jewish state stand, could it survive against so many odds? Would the Great Powers come to its defense, if only to redeem themselves? Or would Israel be nothing but a spasm in history? The enemy had proclaimed a holy war and six hundred thousand Jews were already fighting, without arms or experience, against six armies at once, demonstrating a desperate, lucid courage two thousand years old.

The discussions were long and inexhaustible. My teacher,

an old man famous for his Talmudic knowledge, pulled me into a corner and asked me point-blank: "From now on will you believe in miracles?"

"Yes," I answered.

"And you'll no longer deny God's blessings?"

"No."

His piercing eyes were watching me, his voice had become harsh and insulting: "Well, then, young man, it takes very little to please you."

"The rebirth of a sovereign nation extinct for twenty centuries, you consider that little?"

I had never seen him so angry with me. "You don't understand," he said, enunciating each word carefully. "There is Israel and there is your reaction to Israel. I am thankful to Israel, but you disappoint me. The present and the future make you forget the past. You forgive too quickly."

I blushed. Four years earlier I had left my town and my studies to enter night. Like many Jews from many towns in occupied Europe, I had gone carrying the name of the Messiah on my lips, the very same name which, according to legend, had preceded creation. I believed in man and even more in what transcended him. Then, abruptly, all my ties were cut. Overnight I was robbed of even the smallest point of reference and support. I was confronted with emptiness. Everywhere. To avoid sinking, I needed a miracle, or at least a sign.

"No!" my teacher was shouting. "I have no right to refuse salvation, though it does indeed come too late for too many. I am prepared to welcome it and open for it as many doors and hearts as possible. That, yes. But call it miraculous, that I refuse. We have paid too dearly for it.

To be a miracle, it would have had to happen a little sooner."

And, with clenched teeth, he began to pray, while in Israel blood was already flowing.

I often think of that conversation. I think of it each time I visit the Holy Land, each time I hear of an intrinsic link connecting the national resurrection of Israel to the era of Auschwitz. Everything inside me rebels against such a juxtaposition, particularly when viewed not as a purely chronological consequence but as a compensation or process of cause and effect. Actually, the two experiences have in common only those who lived through them. Thence their relationship on the level of conscience and sensitivity, perhaps even of memory, but not in any pattern of history. To impose a logical sequence on Auschwitz and Jerusalem, or a design other than dialectical, would be to diminish both.

Israel, an answer to the holocaust? It is too convenient, too scandalous a solution. First, because it would impose a burden, an unwarranted guilt-feeling, on our children. To pretend that without Auschwitz there would be no Israel is to endow the latter with a share of responsibility for the former. And second, Israel cannot be an answer to the holocaust, because the holocaust, by its very magnitude, by its essence too, negates all answers. For me, therefore, these are two distinct events, both inexplicable, unexplained, mysterious, both staggering to the mind and a challenge to the imagination. We shall never understand how Auschwitz was possible. Nor how Israel, scarcely a few years later, was able to draw from itself the strength and vision to rebuild its home in a world adrift and in ruins.

Certainly, after Auschwitz, the Jews needed a call to consolation, or at least a diversion. To breathe. To regain courage. But the world at large needed it even more. To make us forget its silence, its overwhelming complicity. To buy itself a clear conscience, and thereby, perhaps, escape its own destruction. In other words: the Jewish people would have continued to exist even if it had had to wait fifty more years to reclaim its state. Not so the world. The world, crushed with guilt, could not afford to wait.

Let us be more specific: had Zionism and its demands not existed, what would have become of the survivors of the ghettos and the camps, the partisans emerging from the forests and mountains who, according to all logic, should have scorned the human race and dedicated themselves to hating and despising it. Outraged, betrayed, these men and women, disowned and victimized by society, had the right and also the means to pledge themselves to nihilism and let their anger explode—come what may. They had nothing to lose, no one to spare. No ties to country or life. No more illusions about the trend of history or man. They could easily have become social misfits, even criminals. Had they set fire to all of Europe, no one would have been surprised. But they did not.

They did not even take the opportunity to wreak vengeance on their avowed executioners. This cannot be repeated often enough: after the German debacle, the survivors wished to be neither avengers nor inquisitors.

They might easily have become one or the other by releasing their pent-up rage. Instead, they let themselves be caught up in the great political and messianic adventure held out by Palestine; they devoted to it all their energy, all their ambition. Nothing else mattered any more. The struggle demanded all their passions, all their dedication. That is why there was no settling of accounts.

This also explains the almost unanimous sympathy shown to the newly created Jewish state at that time. In a vague way, people were grateful to Israel for having come into being just in time to divert the lightning. This was equally true for Western countries and the so-called people's democracies: Israel transcended the Iron Curtain. Stalin and Truman each claimed the honor of being first to establish diplomatic relations with Tel Aviv. Prague gave Israel arms and planes. At the United Nations, Andrei Gromyko, Russia's seasoned tactician, was on hand at every critical moment to support Israeli positions. France granted free passage to immigrants and volunteers. Public opinion was favorable, enthusiastic: people saw in Israel a promise, a symbol and an encouragement. The intelligence of its farmers, the courage of its fighters, its determination to conquer the desert and build there a new bastion of hope, a new city of sunshine and reward: one admired its work, one blessed its vision and pioneering spirit; not to love it meant to diminish oneself.

How far away it all seems now. Old friends falter, others turn hostile. Like the Jewish people throughout the centuries, the Jewish state today stands alone and must continually justify its existence. Not a day goes by without its "case" being examined and tried. By the right and the left. And by professional neutrals and pacifists of every stripe. Israel is criticized for its stubbornness; its enemies are not. It is reproached for its victories, and what preceded and provoked them is forgotten. Under the pretext of anti-Zionism, young German anarchists engage in active anti-Semitism. Chinese, Russians and Algerians train and equip Arab terrorists to kill and be killed. Then come the "revolutionaries" among Western intellectuals, who create an aura of romance around air-piracy and air-killings, thereby succeeding in conducting "guerrilla" warfare by remote control. A saddening and grotesque phenomenon surpassed only by the one we witness in Poland: an anti-Semitism without Jews.

All this explains why, though I am not a citizen of Israel, I totally identify with its destiny. In its solitude, Israel represents for me not an answer but a question, and even more than that: a reappraisal. It does not help me to understand the holocaust. On the contrary: in view of Israel, I understand Auschwitz less than before.

Question mark for a world it baffles, Israel is a question also in relation to its own history. I make it mine, just as I make mine Israel's determination to transform the hate imposed upon it into a craving for solidarity with the world. A world still dominated by hate. This is a miracle in itself, the only one perhaps.

But Israel, for me, also represents a victory over absurdity and inhumanity. And if I claim it for myself, it is because I belong to a generation which has known so few.

POSTWAR: 1967

W E SHOULD HAVE EXPECTED
it. The world begrudges Israel its victory. Its lightning
campaigns against four armies and some twenty nations
were won too quickly and too spectacularly. To have won
at all was bad enough. The world is puzzled. A victorious
Israel does not conform to the image and destiny certain
people want to assign to it. They would rather see it defeated, on its knees, a victim of error or injustice, whatever;
and be ready to rescue it later, mourn it, cover it with
wreaths and eulogies exuding charity and perhaps even
love. A Jew triumphant over death? An intolerable
thought, even for its so-called protectors. They love the
Jew only on the cross; if he is not there yet, well, they can
oblige. And venerate him afterwards.

Judging by the trend of opinion emerging clearly in
certain quarters, it would appear that the world cannot
forgive the Jew for having disappointed it: the promised
holocaust will not take place. The lamb dares refuse the
sacrifice. A distinct lack of manners on his part. And those
tears ready to flow on his grave, that pity ready to be be-
stowed on the unfortunate survivors, they are useless now,
and by his own fault. Worse: in a paroxysm of ingratitude,
not content merely to have escaped the massacre, the Jew

finds ways to humiliate those who prepared it. After all, he could have handled things differently. He could have defeated his enemies without humiliating them. And spared their sensibilities.

And so, the very same people who, before the unleashing of actual military operations, proclaimed Israel's indisputable right to sovereign existence, to survival, to human and national dignity, now turn peevishly against it. They feel frustrated because Israel should have known "how far one may go too far." Most vociferous are those who yesterday were still ready to disregard, temporarily, of course, their avowed policies, political or other loyalties, and take up its defense. Certain so-called liberal Jews, traditional defenders of oppressed peoples, threatened minorities and liberation movements, do not conceal their remorse at having let themselves raise their voices in behalf of their besieged people during the days of anguish and uncertainty. Yesterday's impulse makes them ashamed today.

Let's leave aside the fanatics: they made their choice a long time ago. They follow orders and repeat what they are told. That's nothing new. Why let that bother us? If they choose to set themselves up as eternal judges of history and humanity, that's their concern. They are what they are, and their choices should no longer surprise us. Nor that they insist on treating Israel as aggressor while ignoring the provocations and justifying the acts of war that led to war. For their dialecticians, ideology has always been more important than truth, machines more indispensable than man. To merit their approval, Israel had only to please its enemies by arming itself, if one may say so, with

133

patience, nothing but patience, accepting thereby its role as instrument if not martyr. Israel thought of itself and its own vital interests first, rather than of strings being pulled elsewhere; it is now paying the price. That is the natural order of things. Nobody can thwart the Kremlin's plans and still expect to please the Communists, even the most naïve among them.

The behavior of certain Christians and left-wingers, whose intellectual honesty is above suspicion, is even more painful. Motivated by misplaced humanism, they advance their own thesis: there can be no equating the inflammatory exhortations of a Nasser or a Shukeiry with Israel's armed attack. They freely admit that the Arabs started the war—by blocking the Gulf of Aqaba—but as they see it, the Israeli victory was proof that Nasser had no intention of pursuing it to the end. They will tell you: You know the Arabs, they're like children, they talk a lot, they get excited, one must forgive them, and above all, not take them seriously.

These men who protest their good faith seem to forget that there are words that kill, or at least recall the era of death. Yes, there are words one must no longer use; they are burdened with too many memories. When a Jewish community is threatened with "total war," with blood baths, with extermination by fire, we cannot treat it lightly.

That verbal threats can be dangerous and must be taken seriously, I myself have known for years; I know it even better now that I have seen the planes and tanks in the Sinai, the cannons and rockets, and the soldiers getting ready to use them according to plans—which I have also seen—

drawn up by their general staffs. The immediate objective? To drive the Jews back into the sea. Their leaders have said it and written it, and you will never convince me they did not mean it. You see, I belong to a generation sensitized to the extreme, trained to attach more significance to threats than to promises. It is a fact that in times of danger, our friends and protectors, when in power, suddenly discover in themselves a hypocritical tendency to be cautious and wise. An attitude which emphasizes our solitude. What was true in the past is still true today. During the Six-Day War we witnessed a repetition in history. Only the setting had changed, the mechanism had remained the same. The shadow of Auschwitz finally enveloped Jerusalem. The threatened Jewish state could not count on a single government to help loosen the vise. The policies of de Gaulle in 1967 were worthy of Roosevelt's in 1942: for practical reasons and for the sake of convenience, Jewish destiny was not a decisive factor for either leader.

Why deny it? For us the General's turn-about was deeply shocking and painful. More than anything, it was an emotional disappointment. Israel will manage without French arms shipments: or order arms elsewhere. Suppliers of military equipment abound on both sides of the Atlantic. It is on the human level that France's official defection hurts most. Many of us had continued to see in the hero of June 18, 1940, not just "a friend and ally" on whose word one could depend, but also a conscience. So much for that: we should not have been so naïve.

Again on the human level, stands taken by other public figures have saddened us. I refer to an illustrious writer who, assuming the role of arbiter, sees Israel's victory as a breach in the sacred nature of its mission. The uneasiness

Israel provokes in him is theological. By winning its battles, he seems to think, Israel must be negating its covenant with God.

Does he really believe that the Jews "have chased God out of their land," which is also His land? Does he seriously think that the Holy Land has lost its holiness since the Jews have taken root again? Does he truly feel that a temporal Israel and a spiritual Israel are incompatible?

I saw Israel at war; I can therefore testify in its behalf. In the Old City of Jerusalem, barely reconquered, I saw hardened paratroopers pray and weep for the first time in their lives; I saw them, in the thick of battle, gripped by an ancient collective fervor, kiss the stones of the Wall and commune in a silence as elusive as it was pure; I saw them, as in a dream, jump two thousand years into the past, renewing their bond with legend, memory and the mysterious tradition of Israel. Do not tell me they were moved by a will for power or material superiority. Their will sprang from spirituality and the harrowing immediacy of their past. Their experience was of a mystical nature. Even the non-believers felt transcended by their own acts and by the tales they told about them afterwards. The words on their lips sounded strangely fiery and distant.

It is as if they had all started to believe in miracles, or just—believe. Their moving humility in the face of a victory still unreal in their eyes and mine makes me as proud of them as of their victory.

A curious victory in other ways too. No celebration to mark it, no ceremony. The transition went almost unnoticed. No military parades, no public rejoicing. The conquerors of Sinai and the liberators of Jerusalem, the very same who had held the world in suspense, I saw them return to their homes and resume their work as if nothing had happened. Their alleged desire to dominate seemed aimed only at their own pride; which they did dominate, though they had every right to it. Humanity has never known victors less arrogant, heroes more sober and eager for peace and purity.

That their victory should give rise to envy I can understand. But it is wrong to reproach them for it. They needed it to survive. So did we.

MOTTA GUR

Colonel Mordecai Gur— known to his friends as Motta—turns his shrewd, questioning gaze on me.

"No, I'm not religious . . . Of course not. Why should I be? And why do you ask?"

"No special reason."

His face is tense and deeply lined, but his eyes sparkle with mischief. My answer does not satisfy him. He repeats: "But why do you want to know?"

"I heard you on Kol Israel."

. . . The fighting barely over, several unit commanders had gone on the air to comment on its various phases and implications. The radio broadcast of Motta Gur, liberator of the Old City of Jerusalem, was so successful, it had to be repeated several times.

"Your tale," I tell him, "had a certain dimension—forgive me if I insist—a religious dimension."

He stares at me in mock exasperation. What was I trying to prove? Now it's his turn to question me: "Did I speak of God?"

"No."

"Of the Bible?"

"No, you didn't."

"Did I discuss problems other than those relating directly to the fighting? Did I preach faith? Did I quote the Torah?"

"No."

"So you see! Your question is absurd. Ask anyone you want, but not me. All I did was tell a story. Mine."

True. But what a story! There is prophecy in it, and the more I listen to it, the more I like what I hear. Feverish preparations, mounting tension, orders and counterorders, terse telephone conversations, errands, details, muffled voices and hurried steps in the night: the final stage before the first attack. Gripped by a boundless fervor, disobeying orders, heedless of danger, every paratrooper in the battalion wanted to fight in the front line, at the very eye of the storm. The colonel led the way. His driver, a giant named Ben-Tzur, kept jamming the accelerator to the floor, yet Motta Gur was shouting: "Faster, Ben-Tzur, faster!"

Once they were forced to stop because of an overturned Jordanian motorcycle, probably mined. "Ben-Tzur, what are you waiting for? Keep moving!" There was no mine. At the entrance to the Old City, a half-open gate, perhaps a trap. "Go on, Ben-Tzur, move!" It was not a trap. Jumping out of the jeep—useless in the narrow alleyways—the colonel started running with the others, ahead of the others. A wild, insane race. Shells ripping through the waning night. Men blown to bits. The wounded among them moaning and crawling ahead on their knees. The paratroopers were running from street to street, from turret to turret, propelled by an irresistible, unrelenting force, every one of them obscurely aware of having lived for this moment, for this race. And suddenly, over the deafening clangor, Motta Gur was shouting his report to

Headquarters: "The Har Habayit is ours! Do you hear me? The Temple Mount is in our hands . . ." And everywhere, on every front, in every home, officers and soldiers, children and old people wept and embraced. And in those tears, those explosions of feeling, there was an element of the unreal which made the event unique, and changed all those who lived through it.

"You make it sound too poetic," says Motta Gur. "I don't buy that."

"In other words, for you, this was just another episode, another battle among many?"

"I wouldn't go that far . . . After all, it was Jerusalem, wasn't it? But . . . why are you laughing?"

"And in what way was Jerusalem different from any other military objective?"

"Jerusalem was not just a military objective. It was something else. Jerusalem is . . . Jerusalem."

"And what makes Jerusalem . . . Jerusalem?"

"Its history, of course. It's Jewish, isn't it? It touches me. It concerns me."

"Jericho too has a history linked to ours. And so does Hebron. And Gaza. And Bethlehem."

"Your comparisons are boring. Jerusalem defies comparison."

He has fallen into the trap. Here he is, expressing himself in mystical terms. He realizes it and falls silent. As for me, I visualize again the unforgettable: his paratroopers in front of the Wall.

"Your men were sobbing like children. And you? Did you cry?"

"No."

"You didn't?"

"I arrived at the Wall somewhat after my advance unit. I was busy elsewhere. The battle had to go on." And after a silence: "And then . . . I don't like ceremonies."

"None?"

"I like simplicity, spontaneity."

Should I now express my view that he would have liked the encounter with the Wall for precisely that reason; for its disorder and total lack of stagecraft? No need for words. He knows. Because, once more, he is on the defensive:

"Let's change the subject, shall we?"

"No."

He shrugs his shoulders.

"All right," I say. "We won't talk about the Wall. Let's talk about something else. The Temple Mount, for example. You were the first to get there, weren't you?"

"Yes," he says, stiffening again.

I look him straight in the eye and ask: "Were you moved?"

"I'll let you guess."

"Moved . . . to tears?"

"I didn't cry."

"You didn't?"

"Stop bothering me, will you? I don't believe in tears. Period."

"Just the same, try to remember: standing there, on the reconquered Mount, what did you feel? Pride? A sense of victory? Nostalgia, perhaps?"

"Let's say: a feeling no words can express."

"Try."

"One must not speak of things one feels deeply."

"Then, what should one speak of?"

"Nothing."

"I don't agree. Whosoever survives a test, whatever it may be, must tell the story, that is his duty."

Motta Gur reflects and acquiesces reluctantly: "Perhaps. You may be right." His eyes half-closed, he seems to be rummaging in his memory. "You may be right, but I could not satisfy your curiosity. I could not define the feeling that swept through me at that particular moment. I only remember how deep it was. Never, in all my life, have I felt anything so powerful, so exhilarating."

Then he lowers his voice to tell me his dream.

A dream which, after 1948, was to haunt more than one Jewish fighter: to recapture what was once the capital of the Kingdom of Israel and reunite it with Israel's destiny.

"For twenty years, always and everywhere, I was preparing myself for that certain day, that certain battle. You see, when the Old City capitulated, I was posted in the Negev. And I promised myself one thing: the next time, at the first opportunity, I would be the one to lead the assault. One day I even said it—jokingly—to Chief Army Chaplain Shlomo Goren: 'You stick with me and I guarantee you will see the Wall again before anyone else.' When we met in the Temple court, in front of the Wall, he reminded me of my promise."

"But you, had you forgotten it?"

"Forgotten it? You'll laugh, but I never doubted I would

keep my pledge. Listen: just a few days before Monday, June 5th, I suddenly decided it might be useful to take my staff on an inspection tour of Jerusalem's outposts. When, in fact, we had no business there. According to the plans, my objective was a point behind the Egyptian lines, to the south and rather far."

"How, then, do you explain this improvised inspection?"

"I can't. Not even to myself. I felt like going to Jerusalem, so I went. To see. To familiarize myself with the terrain. You never know what can happen; it's best to be prepared."

And then all hell broke loose in the desert. Israel had been fighting for several hours, yet Motta Gur and his paratroopers, though in a state of alert, still did not know that they would be assigned the privileged task the government itself hesitated to envision seriously. It all depended on young King Hussein: would he adopt a "wait and see" policy or would he open a second front? By committing the most fatal error of his reign, the Jordanian sovereign invited Motta Gur and his troops to enter history.

"And you were sure of victory?"

"I was."

"From the beginning?"

"From the beginning."

"You never doubted it?"

"Never."

And he explains: he knew the respective strengths of his own men and the enemy's. The Jewish soldiers were better trained and motivated; for them it was a matter of defending their children and their homes. They could be trusted never to give up without a fight, nor would they ever retreat, leaving behind functioning tanks and cannons.

"Would you say they're fearless?"

"Everybody experiences fear sometime."

"You too?"

"Yes. I too."

"Fear of suffering? Of dying? Of dying one hour before victory?"

"Just fear."

"Does it make you feel ashamed?"

"Not at all. Fear is human. Even if I could discard it, I don't think I'd want to. It's the price I want to and must pay. However, it is easier to overcome by putting yourself on the firing line rather than sending your men, your comrades. Many times I would have preferred to be with them or in their place. I would imagine them wounded, disfigured, and envy them their fear."

Abruptly he falls silent, a vision of horror in his eyes. This hardened officer, who wishes he were made of steel, worries about the fate of his soldiers to the point of pain, of tenderness. In mid-battle he remembered a captain he knew to be profoundly religious. Imagining what his joy would be to see the Wall again, he dispatched him on the spot: the captain arrived there before his commanding officer.

"Strange," says Motta Gur, wrinkling his forehead. "Though begun as a strictly military operation, the conquest of Jerusalem changed character. Suddenly, the way we fought was different: we were different. Overwhelmed by a feeling at once new and ancestral, we understood that our true objective was no longer the taking of this strategic position or that important network, it was the liberation of history itself. We were on our way to keep an appointment, and we went running, breathless, our hearts pounding . . ."

But above all, don't tell him that he expresses himself more like a storyteller than a soldier. Tell him that his tale is inspired, and he'll fly into a rage.

"You're really mad! Inspired, me? I'm not even religious and certainly not observant! Haven't I said it often enough? If from time to time I happen to go to the synagogue, what does that mean? That my children go and I accompany them. And what does that prove? Nothing, except that I fulfill my duty as a father . . ."

No, Motta Gur is not religious, at least not in the usual sense. If I detect ancient sounds of legend in his narrative, is that his fault? If I hear echoes of the Talmud in his tales, is that his fault?

"Listen," he says, and now he is really upset, "don't let your imagination run away with you. Understand? I have told you once and I'll tell you again: I fought a battle, that's true. But I only did my duty as a soldier and as a Jew. And now, here with you, I've done nothing but tell a story. Mine."

Wrong! It is also the story of a dream. His, ours. And the dream transcends the story.

TO A CONCERNED
FRIEND

You are concerned. That is what you told me when last we met. Concerned about the situation in the Middle East, naturally. So am I. Concerned and troubled. The future seems forbidding. Cease-fire violations, artillery duels, sabotage and reprisals, night raids, assaults and bombardments: violence negates inertia and fosters its own escalation. Too many mothers, on both sides, are in mourning. Too many young, on both sides, give their lives before having lived. Will, then, this curse never be revoked? I thought: We are friends, you and I, we share the same faith in friendship, surely we share the same fears. Except that you went on to say: I should not like Israel to become a power defined by its conquests, and yet that is bound to happen. You added: I would not like to see the young Jews over there developing a conqueror's mentality and yet, barring a dramatic change, they may indeed be forced to acquire such a mentality.

And so, since we are friends, I write to reassure you. You are wrong to worry; you needn't. The Jew in victory will not disappoint you: he remains unchanged, even under changing conditions. He may no longer be victim, yet he will never be tormentor. He will not try to break the will of enemies in his power by means of gallows and/or humiliation. Victory, in the Jewish tradition, does not depend on defeat inflicted on the adversary. Every victory is first a victory over oneself. For this reason too the Jew has never been an executioner; he is almost always the victim.

Walk about on the Western Bank and you will feel neither the horror nor the pity inevitably inspired by European ghettos. No degrading images of hunger and desolation. The sick are cared for, the children fed. Also, people here are free. Free to go wherever they wish, see whomever they wish. The local dignitaries will speak overtly of their opposition to Israel: they know they won't be punished. Just as they may listen to broadcasts from Cairo or Damascus, which day after day incite them to terrorism and rebellion. Do you know many examples of occupation forces permitting such practices? Do you know of other cases where the occupier encourages the occupied to maintain family, commercial and other ties with the enemy while still in a state of war? Go and see what is happening on the Allenby Bridge—where hundreds of residents shuttle daily between Hebron, Nablus, Bethlehem and Amman—and you will no longer compare the situation in Israel today with conditions that prevailed in German-occupied Europe.

Of course, you will answer me that, by definition, every occupation regime is saddening and fundamentally unjust. That is my opinion too. Only I feel compelled to add this: since for the moment the occupation is necessary, the form it takes in Israel is, I believe, the most humane and least oppressive possible. It is an act of bad faith to compare Israeli soldiers to Germans; theirs is another concept of man and his triumphs.

Why should you expect Jewish fighters to reveal a sudden thirst for power, for violence, when in the heat of battle they remained calm and sober? Why should you expect them to develop, belatedly, sadistic inclinations?

Don't forget: this Six-Day War, this victory, Israel did not want them. They were imposed on her. Nor should you forget that hostilities did not erupt overnight. It was neither chance nor whim. For three weeks—and this cannot be stressed enough—Israel faced psychological warfare on a terrifying scale. The departure of the United Nations Emergency Force, the blockade of the Tiran Straits, the troop movements into Sinai, the military alliances, the inflammatory slogans, the unleashed mobs prodded by destructive, vengeful madness. Take another look at Arab propaganda of those days, including Ahmed Shukeiry's vociferations. And don't tell me he behaved like an "irresponsible imbecile": Nasser and Hussein considered him respectable enough to embrace before cameras and include him in their war councils. And all together proclaimed the hour of punishment to be near: the name and the people of Israel were to be destroyed by fire and brimstone.

With such shouts of hate in his ears, any other fighter would have sought revenge. But the Jewish soldier knew how to control himself. The prisoners-of-war, who expected the worst, namely, the fate they had reserved for the Jews, were as astounded by the moderation of the victor as by his victory. Same astonishment in the civilian Arab population. With few exceptions, the victims-to-be of yesterday did not allow their accumulated, repressed bitterness to turn into cruelty. There were no lootings, no rapes, no collective ransoms, no executions of hostages. Nor any of the scenes of savagery that ordinarily accompany territorial conquest.

Listen to a story heard from a friend. I vouch for its sincerity and authenticity.

This friend belonged to one of the battalions sent to liberate the Old City of Jerusalem. The battles were grim and bloody. Suddenly, under a rain of deadly shells, in a narrow little street just taken, an Arab called out to a patrol and asked to see an officer: it was urgent. Thinking the man might be a truce emissary or a double agent, my friend received him.

"I need a doctor," the Arab shouted. "Quick, my wife is about to give birth."

The officer almost burst into laughter, so absurd were both the request and the situation. He hesitated—and I like him for that hesitation—weighing the facts. Who deserved priority? His men, wounded and in pain, or that unknown woman whose child—a son?—might one day grow up to stab his own son? He finally made a decision—and I like him even more for that: a Jewish doctor was sent to assist the woman in labor.

Why would you expect this officer, returned to civilian life, to discover in himself, now, an inclination toward brutality, an instinct for torture?

Permit me, at the risk of shocking you, to go to the heart of the matter: if today so many genuine or pseudo pacifists, so many politicians speak out against Israel's victory, it is precisely because the Israelis won without sacrificing their honor. Had the victorious Jew behaved normally, that is, in the manner of other conquerors of recent times, had he too established a master-slave or man-object relationship with the vanquished, he would have been understood and forgiven. What the world cannot forgive Israel is her determination, both daring and irritating, to remain human in a situation which is not.

An example: the Old City of Jerusalem, yes, Jerusalem again. During the twenty years of its illegal occupation by Jordan—in defiance of United Nations resolutions—no one raised any objection. It was considered a *fait accompli.* No government deemed it opportune to protest against the profanation of Jewish holy places, the construction of luxury hotels on ancient Jewish cemeteries, the demolition of synagogues several centuries old. Members of the U.N. accepted with equanimity the fact that Jordan violated its own armistice agreements by forbidding Jews access to the Wailing Wall. But as soon as the Jews replaced the Jordanians as custodians of the sacred city, the reactionary and communist governments, left-wing editorial writers and right-wing propagandists voiced their indignation. The injustices suffered by Israel? Her inherited rights vested in a past three thousand years old? Arguments of no interest. The fact that no Arab was chased out of the Old City in 1967, while all Jews were expelled from it in 1948, does not count. Neither does the fact that Israelis respect, and guarantee respect for, the holy places of all three religions for the first time since the destruction of the Temple. On the contrary, I tell you it works against them: it is because Israelis commit no sacrilege and profane no mosques, that they are resented.

Would you like another example? The raid on the Beirut airport. Remember? A dozen planes destroyed on the ground: a brilliant operation against Lebanon, whose authorities had been closing their eyes to the activities of Palestinian terrorists. Remember the international outcry? Never was the Security Council convened so hurriedly to vote so quickly, so unanimously so severe a condemnation. The Arabs' friends were enraged; Israel's, confused and embarrassed. Even pro-Israeli circles rejected our thesis that twelve planes were not as valuable as the life of the one man assassinated by Arab terrorists, one week earlier in Athens.

At the time I couldn't help but wonder: Why was everyone up in arms? Why more than usual? In what way was this relatively innocuous and bloodless reprisal different from the others? Why did it encounter such lack of understanding, since it involved no loss of human life? And, as usual, the answer was inherent in the question: the Beirut raid was condemned *because* it had caused no bloodshed. Had there been human casualties, the reaction would have been less violent. By affirming that man—any man—is more important than objects—any objects—Israel alienated public opinion. Please, do not protest: that's how it is, that's how it has always been. People used to hate the Jew because he refused to fit their concept of a victim. Today they are disturbed because he refuses to fit their concept of a victor. He has dared to undertake, and successfully, a perilous operation—the temporary seizure of an enemy airport—without causing a single injury. Admit that there is something in that to offend his judges.

Actually, we ought not to be surprised. For as long as the Jew has existed, he has been judged. At first, by God. Then, by men who, one after the other, using different titles and pretexts, insisted on substituting themselves for God. Finally, each Jew had to justify himself in the eyes of the entire world for each day, each hour that he was still alive. And the game goes on. He is rebuked for his nationalism and his universalism, his wealth and his poverty, his submissiveness and his revolt. We have not yet finished pleading on behalf of the Jews who during the holocaust accepted death without a fight, and already we are forced to defend other Jews who, one generation later, do fight— and fight well—because they refuse to die.

But then, who are our judges? Moscow, whose armies invaded Prague? Washington, whose troops razed Vietnamese villages "in order to save them," as one officer put it? The saints with clean hands in Paris and London? Formosa? It would be a farce, were it not for its tragic aspects. Read the papers, my friend. Thousands of human beings are dying in the jungles of Asia. And the United Nations keeps silent. Entire tribes are being wiped out in Sudan, Yemen and Indonesia. And the United Nations keeps silent. Political analysts speak of nuclear wars as possibilities—who will be the first to pull the trigger? against whom?—nobody cares. U Thant has indicated he does not wish to be disturbed at home except in case of war. And nobody is even perturbed. In Biafra—remember?—children ravaged by hunger and disease looked at press photographers one day, one minute before dying. And the United Nations kept silent. Wait, my friend. May I add to that last sentence. I recently heard over the radio that the number of Biafrans dead of hunger—yes, of hunger—has reached, and probably exceeded, two million. And the United Nations kept silent. The item was not even placed on the agenda.

When do the distinguished delegates wake up? When they are instructed to indict Israel. When Israel is on trial, everybody stand up to be counted. Then all have something to say. Why are they so eager? Because, to them too, Israel remains a people apart, a people whose very existence constitutes a challenge to richer and mightier nations. Whose way of conducting wars and winning them is a reproof to those whose own battles brought no glory to the human spirit.

To me, Israel's victory is above all a moral one. A state without a one-party system, without summary executions—do you know of many in that part of the world? In Baghdad, festive crowds dance from night to dawn beneath the gallows. In Egypt, concentration camps are still realities. And do you know how the Syrians treat their Jewish prisoners? They drive them mad—literally mad—with torture.

In Israel, the arbitrary does not rule; the judiciary is free from pressure. Dissent is every citizen's right. As yet, no one has been condemned for speaking his mind in public. The opposition sits in Parliament and not in jail. Palestinian terrorists in Nablus and Gaza enjoy more rights than do Houari Boumedienne's adversaries in Algiers. In Israel, revolution has not eliminated democracy, national independence has not been achieved at the price of human dignity. That is her true victory.

Of course, like you, I hope with all my heart that one day, Jew and Arab, reconciled for the sake of their children, will live in peace, without the aspirations of the one limiting the other's. That this reflects the deepest vision

of the Israelis, I firmly believe. Threatened by their own
extremists, Arab leaders unfortunately do not dare take
the hand extended them, and therein lies the tragedy.
Were they to accept one first contact, the rest would become possible. Instead, they insist on denying Israel's
very existence: peace cannot be made with what does
not exist. A blindness as childish as that is inadmissible.
Granted that a nation, like a man, may, in a surge of
madness, hate and fight another nation. But to deny the
existence of the other or regard it as a non-nation
peopled with non-persons is unacceptable. Even God
does not permit Himself to reduce man to object. Israel
therefore has no choice: she will wait until she is recognized. Remember: twenty centuries of solitude have taught
her the secret of waiting.

Frankly, I know what really worries you. You
are afraid that what you call "the Jewish soul," forged
in suffering and accustomed to persecution, will stop
being Jewish. You fear that without its wounds, it may
change and become cruel, inhuman: like the world it faces.
Well, rest assured; the Jewish soul has withstood so many
onslaughts of hate, an ancestral hate which has worn many
faces, that it will find it easy to resist the fleeting thrill of
military glory. Have faith, Israel deserves it: our history
is the best proof. A soul does not change so radically and
so quickly. The mentality, the instincts of a conqueror
are not acquired in months, or even years; it takes generations, and implies a tradition the Jews do not claim. The
Jew who has resisted change throughout his millennial

history, do you really suppose he would repudiate his heritage because of a few victories on the battlefield?

You know and esteem the Jewish people enough to realize that the secret of its survival—and the antagonism this survival arouses—is linked to its unrelenting will not to assume a destiny other than its own. The setting and circumstances are immaterial. For the duration of its torment, the Jewish soul has remained Jewish—that is, vibrant to everything human—and Jewish it will remain now that we can see a glimmer of light.

TO A YOUNG GERMAN
OF THE NEW LEFT

"... *A*ND THIS IS WHY *at the end of this battle, from within this town which has taken on the face of hell, above and beyond all the tortures inflicted on our people, in spite of our maimed dead and our villages of orphans, I can tell you that at the very moment we are about to destroy you without pity, we nevertheless feel no hate for you. And even if tomorrow we should have to die like so many others, we still would feel no hate.*"

With these words, written in 1944, Albert Camus addressed himself to a German who might have been your father. I quote them to you today because they bear directly on what we face today. As in 1944, the issue is hate. Yours. Directed against me. Against us.

Lately, much has been written about it in the press. You are, after all, rather noisy. Like so many youngsters who confuse lack of discipline with independence, you have tantrums and destroy everything in sight. So that we cannot help hearing you; you force us to listen.

Not a week goes by without my reading about you in the news. Riots in Berlin: instigated by you. Violence in Frankfurt: you again. Marches, demonstrations, rebellions: you, always you.

Incidentally, we are not complaining. We consider it natural and, in a certain sense, desirable that you should feel the need to challenge the regime—whatever it may be —and reject authority—whatever its source.

Your impulse to rebel, to the degree that it is genuine and pure and therefore implies a need for innocence, merits approval. More than anyone else you have the right, perhaps even the duty, to direct your outcry of despair and disgust toward your parents and the world they are handing down to you.

More than anyone else you have a right to be angry, you who were born after the deluge, after the accounting, into a blemished world, into the midst of a fanaticized and stubborn people that repudiated its Führer only after his military defeats and not for his crimes.

The important book of this era, a book of horror and malediction, you are the one who could write it: the son accusing the father of having mutilated and poisoned his future even before giving him birth.

In this respect, you are less fortunate than we. You see, we have no reason to hate our fathers. You, on the contrary, have many. You cannot hope for brotherhood without hating your elders for having killed all hope; you cannot proclaim faith in mankind without repudiating them for having debased that faith. Not to despise your guilty fathers would make you inhuman. And unworthy of redemption.

There was a time when I thought I too could, and must, hate your fathers. I was against the cheap liberalism that requires one to forget and forgive—and absolve—for the sake of political or religious expediency. Whoever loves his executioner, I thought, creates a dangerously false vision of love and a dangerously unreal image of man. Whoever kills out of love, or simply with love, must in the end kill that love. He who feels pity for the cruel, says the Talmud, will eventually be cruel to those capable of pity. For man, condemned to choose between the roles of torturer and victim, love and what negates love may not be combined; no mortal has the right to reconcile them. It is one or the other, one against the other. Murder, by its own definition, excludes the human element of promise. Assassination—as end, not as means—constitutes an assault against the immortality pledged to man. Who kills, kills God. It is not enough, therefore, to fight murder and murderer; one must also cut all ties with them and relegate both behind walls of hatred. That is what I thought.

With the passing years one learns that feelings, like persons, escape us. In time, the most vital sources run dry. Even love, even hate. Reviving the one is no less disappointing than plunging back into the other. We thought we carried within ourselves dormant volcanoes; they are burned out. Who knows? Perhaps "to hate" like "to love" may be conjugated only in the present tense.

But for you, things are different. Whether we, as Jews, choose to forgive or to wait, that is our concern. Either way, it does not solve your problems. Forgiveness is not yours to give, especially not to your fathers, whose names and disgrace you bear. You cannot help but ask certain questions and demand certain explanations they can neither answer nor explain.

Born of so much anger, out of so many ruins, your revolt seems valid because it implies the need to repent, the desire to atone. Unfortunately you are not aware of its limitations. Originating in excessive trauma, it strives for equally traumatic and excessive goals.

Refusing to limit your criticism to your elders, you feel compelled to indict the entire world. Nothing pleases you, no one inspires you. Capitalism, socialism, communism: you abhor *all* systems, you condemn all who attempt to reach you. You detest America because of Vietnam, and Soviet Russia because it does not declare war on America. You consider Western democracies weak and therefore ludicrous: as for the others, you scorn them for being submissive. All countries seem "rotten" and "decadent" to you. The Chinese, it is true, attract you, but only because they are as removed from your "cultural revolution" as you are from theirs.

Never mind. That's your worry. Since you insist on generalizing your rejection, since you persist in alienating all humanity, go ahead, knock your head against the wall; we won't interfere.

But in your childish arrogance you take the liberty of assuming the role of public prosecutor with regard to Israel and the Jewish people. There, I must stop you: you are going too far, you are overstepping the permissible.

First: we have done nothing to hurt you, as far as I know. Second: you still have a fair number of problems to resolve in your own country, in your own self, before meddling with our concerns, which are in no way comparable. Many of your own voices still need to be silenced before you may dare prevent Israeli officials from speaking in public.

How many times must you be told before you understand? Much water will flow through the Rhine and the

Jordan before a nation, any nation, has a lesson, any lesson, to learn from you.

Some of your elders understood this: Heinrich Böll, Alfred Andersch, Martin Walser. They understood that to gain self-respect as men, they had first to earn the respect of their fathers' victims. That is what makes them so human, so close.

Do you know why Günther Grass hesitated many years before visiting Israel? He was afraid of either eventuality: a reception overly hostile, or one overly kind.

He is too lucid and honest to feel totally at ease and free of guilt in the presence of a Jew. And yet he surely has no reason to feel guilty; he did nothing, he was too young. Not only that: his entire body of work is one long outcry of a shattered conscience crushed by burdens imposed by others. That is why his books are so moving, so true. And why I feel a kind of kinship with him; he and I would understand each other. Despite the ghosts clinging to each of us, we could begin a dialogue and give it depth and meaning.

Not with you. Why? Because you are closed to humility. Because you seem not to understand one essential point: that for a German today there is no possible salvation outside his relationship with Jews. Your path will never lead to man unless it leads to us first. Günther Grass realizes this, you do not. You think your hands are clean: so be it. But you also claim to have a clear conscience. There you are wrong.

Is this to say that I subscribe to the theory of collective guilt? Of course not. You are not responsible for the crimes of your fathers. Committed before you were born, the Nazi atrocities concern only their perpetrators. If you yourself are insensitive to them, to the point of ignoring them in your behavior, again that concerns you and only you. Still, you must agree, this lack of sensitivity places you in the present—and the present is your responsibility. It shows you to be someone I should not like to befriend: a heartless creature without memory, and worse, without imagination.

That you should have the impudence to insult Israel in public, and the gall to offer aid and assistance to its enemies: far from releasing you from the German guilt which you discard, these offenses place it firmly on your shoulders. By siding with the Arab terrorists, you define your position within the context of the holocaust. And the time has come for you to know it.

Know at least that you are following your fathers' footsteps. They lived their present under the sign of their hatred for Jews. And so do you: the Jews are not the same, but the hate has not changed, neither has its motivation. Like your fathers, you are against us and for the same reasons. Your propaganda recalls that of Goebbels. He too accused us of wanting to rule the world and oppress all nations. His ally, the former Mufti of Jerusalem, Hadj Amin el Husseini, is still your ally. And you claim to be "progressive"? And "revolutionary," at that? You must be joking. Blind, stubborn reactionaries, that's what you are. What you are doing, your fathers did before you. Though until now you have merely repeated their words, lacking the opportunity to emulate their deeds.

You are responsible for your present activities and doubly responsible to the extent that they relate to the past. In other words, since, after all, twenty-five years have elapsed since Auschwitz, it is impossible—and improper—to judge the present as though it were unrelated to the past. By taking a stand against the Jewish people today, you become guilty of what was done to Jews yesterday. By agreeing to deliver to death the survivors of yesterday's massacres, you become, today, the executioner's accomplice and ally.

So don't go around proclaiming your innocence and your desire to change the world: you have lost that right. You are only carrying on the work planned and undertaken by your fathers. Like it or not, from this moment on, you are their successor and heir.

And now, am I to tell you that I respond to your hate in kind? No, I do not.

Even if you perpetuate the evil spread by your fathers, I shall not hate you. I shall denounce, unmask and fight you with all my power. But your hate will not contaminate me. No, I shall never hate you. Not for yesterday and not even for today. It is something else: for yesterday you have my pity; for today, my contempt.

TO A YOUNG JEW
OF TODAY

Y OU ARE SEVENTEEN and con-
fused. You are Jewish without knowing why. You don't
even know what it means to be Jewish: your friends are
not, and your parents just barely. You are not religious,
yet not fasting on Yom Kippur makes you feel inexplicably
uneasy. You identify with the left, yet reject its anti-
Israeli line: without being a Zionist, you feel as close
to Jerusalem as to Moscow. Marxism attracts you by its
messianic vision, while Jewish messianism leaves you indifferent. Real or apparent, your contradictions trouble
you and you ask me to help untangle them. In short:
what does being a Jew mean in these times and to what
does it commit you? You would like to know.

At the risk of disappointing you, I must confess I have
no key to offer, no secret formula to reveal. Rather than
speak of my certainties—I have so few and they are of
so personal a nature—I prefer to tell you of my efforts to
acquire them. I write in order to understand as much as
to be understood. Reflected in all my characters and their
mirror games, it is always the Jew in me trying to find himself. Perhaps because he is the mirror.

A memory: as a child, I often accompanied my mother
on her visits to the Wizsnitzer Rebbe. Invariably she

solicited the same blessing on my behalf: that I grow up to be a good Jew, fearing God and obeying His Commandments.

Realized in part but only in part, her wish haunts me as does everything linking me to the landscape of my childhood.

Today I already know that God is to be feared, I think I even know why. But I sometimes question the first part of the Rebbe's benediction: how does one become a "good" Jew? It is the adjective that troubles me. Without it, the problem becomes simple.

For to be a Jew, in my eyes, constitutes not a problem—no man is a problem—but a situation. I am Jewish because I am Jewish. And not because my existence is a problem for those who are not. I could never subscribe to Sartre's now obsolete thesis. To tell the Jew that his existence is conditioned from the outside is to negate not only his uniqueness but also his intrinsic identity and creativity. Like man, a Jew defines himself in relation to himself alone. He is subject, not object, a sovereign being, and may not be explained in terms of what he is not and what rejects him.

Must we then conclude that Jewish fate allows no element of choice? Of course not. The two notions are by no means incompatible. On the contrary, to be a Jew, for me, is first to accept my destiny as a Jew, and then to choose it. In other words, we face here a deliberate choice with retroactive effect. It is because I was born a Jew that I can and must choose to be one.

This choice implies an experience on the levels of history and conscience. Nothing is certain, nothing is determined; at any moment, at any turning point, you may begin all over again. You commit yourself totally with your every decision, a commitment that has meaning only to the extent that it springs from an eternally torn conscience, capable of surprising itself.

Ultimately, where does this adventure lead? No Jew can answer. No Jew knows. *Israel nikra holekh,* says the Talmud. The Jew is in perpetual motion. He is characterized as much by his quest as by his faith, his silence as much as his outcry. He defines himself more by what troubles him than by what reassures him.

The Russian, Pushkin once said, is born for inspiration. Unamuno stressed the sober and poetic quality of the Spaniard. To me, the Jew and his questioning are one.

When the debate is over, when everything seems to have been said and accepted, it is then that the Jew appears, and by his very presence, his very survival, reverses learned elaborate theories and doctrines. And one must start anew. Hardly is a structure completed than the Jew insists on altering its foundations. He devises systems and immediately questions their validity; he refuses to be categorized. Small wonder he is not liked: he disturbs and irritates even his protectors. With him, they must be ready for the unexpected. Rooted both in the contemporary and the timeless, he invites hesitation and doubt. He sows disquiet in the heart of the victor and undermines the good conscience of the vanquished. Two thousand years of exile have taught him to wait for the Messiah and to suspect him once he has arrived. Push interrogation to its limits and beyond, and you will do what the Jew has been doing for centuries.

To be a Jew, therefore, is to ask a question—a thousand questions, yet always the same—of society, of others, of oneself, of death and of God. Why and how survive in a universe which negates you? Or: How can you reconcile yourself with history and the graves it digs and transcends? Or: How should you answer the Jewish child who insists: I don't want to suffer, I no longer want to suffer without knowing why. Worse: How does one answer that child's father who says: I don't want, I no longer want, my son to suffer pain and punishment without knowing that his torment has meaning and will have an end? And then, the big question, the most serious of all: How does one answer the person who demands an interpretation of God's silence at the very moment when man—any man, Jew or non-Jew—has greater need than ever of His word, let alone His mercy?

As a Jew, you will sooner or later be confronted with the enigma of God's action in history. Without God, Jewish existence would intrigue only the sociologists. With Him, it both fascinates and baffles philosophers and theologians. Without God, the attempted annihilation of European Jewry would be relevant only on the level of history— another episode in another inhumane war, and what war is not inhumane?—and would not require a total revision of seemingly axiomatic values and concepts. Remove its Jewish aspects, and Auschwitz appears devoid of mystery. Remember Sartre's phrase: in love, one and one are one. For us, contemporary Jews, one and one are six million. Six million times one is God. For just as one cannot conceive of such slaughter with God, it is inconceivable without Him. This is perhaps the final absurdity of the event: all roads lead to it; but all explanations fail. The agony of the believer equals the bewilderment of the non-believer. If God is an answer, it must be the wrong answer. There is no answer. If with the holocaust God has chosen to question man, man is left to answer with a quest having God as object. The interrogation is twofold, and it is up to you to claim it as your own and link it to the actions it calls forth.

But I repeat: we are talking about a double, a two-way, interrogation. It must not be divided. The question man poses to God may be the same God poses to man. Nevertheless, it is man who must live—and formulate—it. In so doing, he challenges God, which is permissible, indeed required. He who says no to God is not necessarily a renegade. Everything depends on the way he says it, and why. One can say anything as long as it is for man, not against him, as long as one remains inside the covenant; only if you repudiate and judge your people from the outside, will you become a renegade.

You will undoubtedly reply: Why speak about God, since I do not believe? Don't worry, my purpose is not to give you back your faith. You are free to replace God with any word—or presence—you prefer. It would in no way alter my message to you.

Besides, I leave you the task of working out your own relationship with God. What matters to me is the relationship between the individual and the community.

To be a Jew is to work for the survival of a people—your own—whose legacy to you is its collective memory in its entirety. No one has the right to dissect history, making personal choices, selecting this period, that personality. Your "I" includes them all. You have seen Moses at Sinai, heard David in his citadel, fought the Romans at Massada, felt the Crusaders' sword. Whoever sees himself as a severed branch becomes *other*, the Midrash teaches us. Isolate yourself within time, and time itself becomes abstraction, and so do you. Time is a link, your "I" a sum total. Your name has been borne by others before you. Your fate is not yours alone. The questions asked by children and the answers they will be given were all heard at Sinai. Your doubts and turmoils, your victories as well, come down to you, in a direct line, from your earliest forebears.

You may call this phenomenon historic consciousness, or spirit of solidarity. Your kinship encompasses those who live in your time and those who survive within you. You cannot fulfill yourself as Jew if you feel no bond with those who share your dilemmas, your celebrations and even your contradictions: the Jews in Israel, in the Soviet Union, in the Arab countries, and even in the lands where they are not harassed.

As a Jew, you are entitled, indeed required, to speak in the name of all Jews. Your word, therefore, takes on immeasurable significance and ancient resonance; it involves others: your ancestors from the most distant past. For the Jew who denies himself denies more than his own person: he denies Abraham, Isaac and Jacob. To betray the present means to destroy the past. Whereas to fulfill oneself means choosing to be a link between past and future, between remorse and consolation, between the primary silence of creation and the silence that weighed on Treblinka.

Because you too have lived the holocaust. You were born after? No matter. One can step inside the fiery gates twenty-five, fifty years later. Do you know Uri-Zvi Greenberg? That Israeli poet and visionary tells the story of a young Jew in King Herod's time who left Jerusalem for

Rome. He had taken along a pillow which remained with him always. One night, as he slept, the pillow caught fire. That very same night the Temple burst into flames in Jerusalem. Yes, one can live a thousand miles away from the Temple and see it burn. One can die in Auschwitz after Auschwitz.

We are all survivors. And since holocaust there was, I prefer not to have experienced it from afar. Does that shock you? With its full burden of distress, shame and horror, the experience the survivor draws from it makes of him a privileged person: a witness.

And do not consider this an attempt to glorify Jewish martyrdom. I do not believe in martyrdom. It belongs to our past, not to our destiny. The Jews never sought to be martyrs; they never equated suffering with sanctity. Asceticism was viewed as alien to our tradition, which sees sin in mortification. Refusal of life and earthly sustenance does not lead to God. God dwells only in joy. God is joy, God is song and fervor. The need to suffer? Invented by those who for two thousand years caused us endless suffering. Martyrdom is only one of many myths attributed to us. It provided our persecutors with a clear conscience, since it permitted them to say: "Yes, we punish the Jews, but it's for their own good, their ultimate salvation." Or: "Our hostility is what keeps them alive." Well, we say: "No!"

The Jews would gladly have forgone the persecutions. Contrary to generally held notions, we do not need anti-Semitism in order to affirm themselves and flourish. We do not need outside stress to enhance our creativity. The image of the hunted Jew, cringing with remorse, finding happiness only in expiation and sacrifice is not of our making.

169

Study it carefully and you will see who created it: our enemies. We attempted to destroy this image as best we could. By laughter. And revolt. Since society considered the Jews' existence incompatible with its own, it was natural that the Jews endeavored to change society. Which explains why so many revolutionary movements, in every sphere, counted so many Jews among their pioneers and apostles.

This brings me back to the question in your letter dealing with the rebellious spirit among your friends. You ask me what your attitude should be.

Rebellion is rooted in the very origins of Jewish history, as you probably learned at school. Abraham breaking his father's idols, Moses rejecting slavery, the prophets criticizing—most disrespectfully—kings and power-seekers: they were true rebels. As were those Jews who, though exiled and oppressed, refused to join the ranks of their oppressors. By their stubborn faith, they contested the validity of the system. Their presence became protest and summons. Each Jew who did not take the easy road of conversion transformed his heresy into an act of defiance. Today's rebellion fits into this pattern. Moreover, I believe it is directly linked to the tragic repercussions of World War II, or more precisely, to the holocaust.

Distrust and rejection of authority, the disturbances and riots, the craving for escape, the urge to abolish uniforms and taboos: the shadow of concentration-camp reality influences the aspirations and actions of your comrades. They may not be aware of it, but even their terms of reference apply more to my generation than to theirs.

It was at Auschwitz that human beings underwent their

first mutations. Without Auschwitz, there would have been no Hiroshima. Or genocide in Africa. Or attempts to dehumanize man by reducing him to a number, an object: it was at Auschwitz that the methods to be used were conceived, catalogued and perfected. It was at Auschwitz that men mutilated and gambled with the future. The despair begotten at Auschwitz will linger for generations.

With Auschwitz in their past, your comrades—Jews and non-Jews alike—rebel against those responsible for this past. Parents, philosophers, teachers, profiteers, opportunists, leaders without ideals, preachers without souls, institutions and organizations without purpose—in short: the discredited and exposed generation of adults that gave you birth. Had it not been so blind, so dishonest, so uninspired, it might have avoided the unleashing of hell, or at least kept some measure of control. By undermining the present, your friends denounce the past, a bankrupt past tottering under its own guilt and revealing anew man's bond to Cain. Every field, every sphere of activity is suspect. A society, a civilization, that could lead to such degradation has, in fact, issued its own verdict, a verdict without appeal.

If your comrades invent new gods, it is because the old ones begot Eichmann and Treblinka. If they lack respect for their elders, it is because the latter lived in the era of Sobibor and Babi-Yar. The anger of the young is a rebuff to the complacency they see in the way their parents choose to live—and die. If they aspire to a new language, it is because their parents' was used in Majdanek. They opt for poverty and anonymity because they want to resemble those who lived in ghettos, and were poorer and lonelier than they will ever be. They allow themselves to be clubbed without responding, so as to follow the example of millions of Jews who, before them, practiced non-violence with the same inefficiency and futility.

You tell me Marx and Engels, Lenin and Stalin no longer inspire your classmates. Why? Because they were part of the system of varied and contradictory ideologies that paved the way for Birkenau, simply by preceding Birkenau. If the new saints are called Mao, Che or Zen, it is only because nothing associates them with the holocaust.

Yes, I remain convinced that the current wave of protest calls into question much more than the present. Its vocabulary takes one back a quarter of a century. Factories and university buildings are "occupied." The Blacks rise up in the "ghettos." Prague is in the headlines and so is Munich. The police use "gas" to disperse demonstrators. Concentration camps in Egypt and in Greece. The Watts and Harlem riots are compared to the Warsaw Ghetto uprising. Biafra is referred to as another Auschwitz. Political analysts talk of nuclear "holocausts." Racism, fascism, totalitarian dictatorship, complicity, passivity: words heavy with past significance, which explains their impact on your comrades. By criticizing today's regimes, they indict yesterday's corruption. That is why it is important to put society on trial, this society which was—and still is—ours. By scorning its defenders, you place yourself on the side of the victims.

But remember: the Jew influences his environment, though he resists assimilation. Others will benefit from his experience to the degree that it is and remains unique. Only by accepting his Jewishness can he attain universality. The

Jew who repudiates himself, claiming to do so for the sake of humanity, will inevitably repudiate humanity in the end. A lie cannot be a stepping stone to truth; it can only be an obstacle.

You ask me: How is one to reconcile man and Jew? The question is badly put. I do not accept the commonly made distinctions between Jew and man; they are not opposites and do not cancel each other. By working for his own people a Jew does not renounce his loyalty to mankind; on the contrary, he thereby makes his most valuable contribution.

More specifically: by struggling on behalf of Russian, Arab or Polish Jews, I fight for human rights everywhere. By calling for peace in the Middle East, I take a stand against every aggression, every war. By protesting the fanatical exhortations to "holy wars" against my people, I protest against the stifling of freedom in Prague. By striving to keep alive the memory of the holocaust, I denounce the massacres in Biafra and the nuclear menace. Only by drawing on his unique Jewish experience can the Jew help others. A Jew fulfills his role as man only from inside his Jewishness.

That is why, in my writings, the Jewish theme predominates. It helps me approach and probe the theme of man.

Of course, had there been no war, I would have sought self-realization in other ways. I would not, for example, have become a writer, or at least, I would have written something other than novels. And in the small yeshiva where I would have stayed, indefinitely poring over the same page of the same book, I would never have imagined one could justify one's existence except by strictly observing the 613 commandments of the Torah.

Today I know this is not enough. The war turned everything upside down, changing the order and substance of priorities. For me, to be a Jew today means telling the story of this change.

For whoever lives through a trial, or takes part in an event that weighs on man's destiny or frees him, is duty-bound to transmit what he has seen, felt and feared. The Jew has always been obsessed by this obligation. He has always known that to live an experience or create a vision, and not transform it into link and promise, is to turn it into a gift to death.

To be a Jew today, therefore, means: to testify. To bear witness to what is, and to what is no longer. One can testify with joy—a true and fervent joy, though tainted with sadness—by aiding Israel. Or with anger—restrained, harnessed anger, free of sterile bitterness—by raking over the ashes of the holocaust. For the contemporary Jewish writer, there can be no theme more human, no project more universal.

As a child I knew all this without really knowing it, and above all, without being able to express it. Yet I still don't know how one becomes a "good" Jew.

A certain Reb Zeira, the Talmud relates, decided to fast a hundred days so as to forget all he had learned. Only afterwards did he go to the Holy Land.

And so what must we do, my generation and yours, to

learn anew what every day, a little more, we tend to forget? I don't know. Throughout this letter I have told you that I attach more importance to questions than to answers. For only the questions can be shared.

RUSSIAN
SKETCHES

As a child I believed that the
Messiah would appear at sunrise, a prince disguised as
beggar, and we would all be present to welcome him: the
rabbis and their disciples, the scribes and their pupils, all
dressed in prayer-shawls and wearing *tephillin*. Some
would sing and dance or recite psalms, others would rejoice and drink from golden goblets filled with wine, the
wine set aside since creation for that precise purpose, for
that precise festivity.

Today I am convinced it will be different. The Messiah
will come at night and will be received with burning
torches and the silence will be such that even the angels in
heaven will stop praising their Master.

The reason for my new belief?

Listen: it happened one Simchat Torah in Moscow, not
too long ago. I have described it before, I shall repeat it,
for the event itself was repeated more than once.

For many hours, thousands of Jewish students had been
dancing in the street leading to the capital's main synagogue. Suddenly the entire block was plunged into darkness. The crowd grew quiet, expecting the lights to go on
again. But soon we realized that they had been turned off

deliberately to end the festivities. Enough dancing, enough singing. Come back next year. Don't overdo your rejoicing.

For a moment there was confusion. Then a mighty roar of protest rose from thousands of throats. No one was willing to accept the implied order. But how does one fight darkness? Here is how: one youngster rolled up a newspaper and lit it. His friends did likewise. The flame was passed from hand to hand. A moment later we were in the midst of a bizarre torchlight parade.

No one had planned it; everything happened by chance. The street became a quietly burning river, a silent stream; its eerie stillness broken only by the crackling of burning paper.

I don't remember how long it lasted. I only remember the dreamlike quality of the scene: students climbing onto a balcony, torches in hand, chanting in Hebrew and Russian: "*Am Israel Hai*, the Jewish people lives and will go on living!" And the crowd answering thunderously: "Hurrah, hurraaah!"

"Well?" asked a man I had met on a previous visit. "What do you think now? Are you more confident than last year?"

I nodded; I had trouble speaking. I recalled a question a close friend had asked me a few months earlier. He had wanted to know whether I still believed, even after the holocaust, in the concept of *netzakh Israel*, the eternity of Israel. And *during* the holocaust? What had my thoughts of Jewish eternity been then? Hadn't I come to the conclusion that we were nearing the end and that soon there would not be even ten Jews left to form a *minyan* in this wicked world?

I had not answered my friend. I wished he were here, standing with me in this joyous, fearless crowd. Here he would answer his own question.

Now you understand what I meant about the coming of the Messiah, who is expected to answer all questions.

He will come at night. And he will be welcomed not only with songs and wine and not only by holy rabbis and their disciples, but also by young Jews expressing their Jewishness by parading with burning torches made of ordinary paper in the very heart of Moscow.

2

This year again there will be dancing and singing in Arkhipova Street in Moscow. Young Jews by the thousands will come and prove to the world that they have not forgotten Simchat Torah and what it symbolizes: a link with Jewish tradition and kinship with the Jewish people.

But this year I shall not be able to join them. For that I am deeply sorry. Since I first visited Russia I have come to think that Simchat Torah cannot be truly celebrated anywhere else. Just as Shavuot reminds us of Sinai and Tishah b'Av of the Temple, Simchat Torah will henceforth be associated with Russian Jewry. More than in Williamsburg, more than in Jerusalem itself, it is in Moscow, not far from the Kremlin, that one feels the depth and magnitude of Jewish commitment to joy and memory. The staunchest Hasid could learn from the most assimilated Jewish student in Moscow how to rejoice and how to transform his song into an act of belief and defiance.

Twice, in consecutive years, I witnessed street-dancing on Arkhipova Street, outside the synagogue. Never before and never since have I felt such elation. Prior to my visit to Moscow, I had not known that Simchat Torah could be more than a holiday: an event and an experience as well.

Since my last visit, changes have taken place in the would, affecting Jewish life everywhere.

The Six-Day War brought about a renewal of the "anti-Zionist" slander campaign in the Soviet press. The infamous Trofim Kitchko has been rehabilitated, reinstated as a member of the Ukranian Academy and even given an important award. His *Judaism Without Embellishment*, once repudiated by world communism, is no longer a source of embarrassment to the Kremlin; on the contrary, his anti-Semitic theories, especially with regard to Israel, seem to have been accepted. So violent were the statements of Soviet representatives in the United Nations, and so frequently were they repeated at home, that there can be no doubt of their being aimed not just at Israel but at Russian Jews as well.

Officialdom embarked on a campaign of intimidation that reached proportions reminiscent of the Stalin days. Synagogue leaders were forced to sign petitions condemning Israel "aggressions." Jews were threatened throughout the Soviet Union and warned to refrain from doing anything that might be interpreted as a move toward identification with Israel and world Jewry.

Too late.

Listen to this story: on June 5, 1967, one of my Israeli friends happened to be in a small town somewhere in Russia. It was early in the morning when he heard the first radio bulletins announcing "Israeli defeats." Since he did not know a soul in that faraway place, my friend, in desperation, decided to find the synagogue. It was already crowded. Hundreds of Jews, young and old, men and women, had gathered spontaneously, as though moved by the same impulse: to be together in a time of danger. When they noticed the visitor and the Israeli emblem in his lapel, they formed a line and each of them came to shake his hand. Some of the older men whispered in Hebrew: "*Al tira avdi Yakov*—do not be afraid, my servant Jacob."

Long after his return to Israel my friend continued to hear the same voices, the same words: for weeks he heard nothing else.

Similar accounts reached us from other cities. When Israel was in danger, the Jews in Russia found ways to express their solidarity. Not all the tales can yet be told. But when the time comes and they are told, they will have the ring of legends. And I wonder: will we be worthy of them?

Are we worthy now of the Georgian Jews who, risking their freedom, send letters to Golda Meir and the United Nations announcing their desire to go and live among their own people in Israel? Or of those youngsters who publicly renounce their Soviet citizenship in order to dramatize their determination to be reunited with their families in Jerusalem, Haifa and Eilat? These acts take courage, just as it takes courage to organize and attend clandestine classes in Hebrew, Jewish history and Jewish literature, or to participate in Simchat Torah festivities.

In Moscow, Leningrad, Tiflis and Tashkent, more and more young people come to sing and dance with more and more enthusiasm each year. They know more and more songs. Here and there, incidents are reported, scores of students are arrested by the police, but the others keep on dancing. Once reawakened, these youngsters, in search of their past, cannot be suppressed. To express what they feel, they are prepared to wait a whole year for one single day, one single night.

Does that mean that they are rediscovering religion? No. They know nothing of Jewish religion, they cannot know. There are no formal Jewish schools, no specially trained teachers. They have nothing. Simchat Torah, for them, is not a religious holiday but something else, and perhaps even something more. For them it is a way, the only way, to identify with *Klal Israel* and enter its history. Therefore, they will not give up. They will go on singing and dancing even if it means imprisonment and reprisals. Simchat Torah represents to them all Jewish holidays combined; on that day and that night, each of them renews his personal covenant with the Jewish people.

They will do it this year too, with new songs and new fervor. But this year I shall not be with them—and for this I cannot but feel guilty.

EXCERPTS
FROM A DIARY

V ERY CLOSE to my Manhattan
apartment, there is a modest Hasidic house of prayer
—a *shtibel*—that reminds me of those I knew in my
childhood. Except that in this one, services are held in
the basement.

The worshippers are mostly refugees. Former residents of Warsaw and its surroundings, they bear
traces of its long hours of agony. All have known the
reality of concentration camps. None speaks of it
except during the holidays. And as I listen, I understand what Rebbe Nachman of Bratzlav meant when
he expressed the wish that his tales be transformed
into prayers.

Passover

Black kaftan, black felt hat, luminous eyes behind
shell-rimmed glasses: Reb Avraham Zemba belongs to the
world of my memories not for his mode of dress alone. He
is pleasant, almost friendly, yet he addresses you only to
let you share a commentary from the *Sfat-Emet* or the
Khiddushei-Harim, pillars of Guerer Hasidism. When he

prays, one sees nothing but his back, yet at times one can almost feel his body tremble.

"On the seventh day of Pesach we all say *Kaddish* here," he tells me. "That was the day we arrived in Treblinka. We were among the last to leave the burning ghetto. In the midst of the uprising, hiding in the ruins, we nonetheless celebrated the Seder. With songs."

And after a silence: "The Midrash relates that Rebbe Hanina ben Dossa prayed with such fervor that without being aware of what he was doing, he would pick up a huge stone and carry it elsewhere."

He never finishes the legend, but in his eyes there is a sorrow so deep and a fervor so ancient that I understand: that stone of Rebbe Hanina ben Dossa now weighs on him, it crushes him, and yet, in his prayers, he does not ask to be relieved of his burden.

Shavuot

Holiday commemorating the revelation at Sinai. The encounter of the people of Israel with the God and Torah of Israel. We stand as we listen to the reading of the Ten Commandments: thou shalt not steal, thou shalt not kill. Naturally, it is always the victims who repeat them.

The reading ended, one of the worshippers makes the customary appeal on behalf of needy Talmudic students. Today it's Yosseph Friedenson's turn. Thin, tense and passionate, a militant orthodox and editor of a Yiddish monthly, he pleads movingly in the students' behalf:

"God has given the Law one time only, yet He asks us to receive it every day. In exchange, all we ask is to be worthy of it."

He stops to clear his throat, and then:

"As a matter of principle and in keeping with tradition, I should now praise the virtues of the Torah. I will not do so, for it would be superfluous. Contemporary history has done it for us by providing irrefutable proof that of all systems, all ideologies, the Torah is the only one that did not betray man. It produced neither camps nor death-factories. Nor do those who adhere to its precepts provoke racial riots or incite to hatred and contempt. They do not see man as object, as obstacle. They denounce no one and seek no vengeance. Their only wish is to devote all their time to the study of Torah. But they do not have the means this requires. Therefore, we must help them. They will not know where the money comes from, nor will we know to whom it goes. Indispensable anonymity on both sides, to avoid vanity and shame . . ."

Curious, this money-collection. Everybody contributes, even though everyone, almost without exception, has difficulty making ends meet. Their generosity reminds me of a humanity that is no more.

Rosh Hashanah

. . . It was in 1944. We had decided to organize a *minyan,* a communal service. A dangerous decision that could easily turn into disaster. But we were determined to welcome the New Year as before, forming a congregation by the sheer force and concentration of our fervor. And the barbed wires? We would have to ignore them. And the jailers? We would have to defy them.

Services took place in a barracks filled to capacity. Even

the *kapos,* even the non-believers, in a rare impulse of solidarity, had decided to be present.

A cantor was found who remembered the Rosh Hashanah service by heart. He recited it aloud and the congregation repeated it verse for verse. We felt like weeping, so great was our self-pity. It was hard, but we controlled ourselves until one of the men, at the end of his endurance, burst into sobs. A moment later everybody was weeping with him. Together, we recalled family and friends, events dating to a time when Europe harbored rabbis and disciples, a thousand synagogues and millions of believers. We reminisced about a past when family meant presence, not separation. We mourned the dead and the living, the vanished homes and desecrated sanctuaries, we wept without shame or hope, and it seemed to us that we would go on weeping until the end of all exiles, until the last breath of the last survivor . . .

Suddenly an inmate stepped forward and began to speak: "Brothers, listen to me. Tonight is Rosh Hashanah, the threshold of a new year. And even though we are starved, in mourning and on the verge of insanity, let us continue our customs and traditions of long ago. In those days, after services, we went up to our parents, our children and friends to wish them a good year. We don't know where they are now, or rather, we do know, which is worse. Let us, nevertheless, pronounce our good wishes—and leave God to transmit them to whomever they belong."

Whereupon the assembly cried out in unison and with all its might, as though wanting to shake heaven and earth: "A good year! A good year!"

And the speaker went on:

"Before we part, we should make the customary *Kiddush*, bless the bread and sanctify the wine. We have no bread; as for the wine, our enemies are getting drunk on it. Never mind, we'll take our tin cups and fill them with our tears. And that is how we will make our *Kiddush* heard before God and His messengers on earth."

. . . And now, many years later, in this humble Hasidic *shtibel*, I watch the same speaker—Shimon Zucker—gently swaying back and forth, during the same Rosh Hashanah service. And I tell myself that one day I shall muster the courage to go to his home and listen to him sanctify the wine and bless the bread.

Yom Kippur

This tale I heard from a morose, but extraordinary old Jew:

On Yom Kippur Eve the dead and the living intermingle. You don't believe it? You say it's superstition? I was like you. And yet . . .

The last Yom Kippur of the war. The entire camp listens as the cantor repeats three times the solemn invocation of *Kol Nidre*. Then comes *Maariv,* followed by the *Vidui,* the confession enumerating all the sins and transgressions a mortal could possibly commit or imagine, from his birth to his death. In the middle of the enumeration an incident occurs. An emaciated inmate, the color of ashes, brutally pushes the cantor aside and addresses the congregation:

"Brothers, I shall not permit you to lie! No, we have not sinned, we have not betrayed, we have not robbed our fellow man! Tonight, for the first time in creation, we are

not the accused, we are the judges. We shall be the ones to
pronounce the sentence. Otherwise, we should be failing
in our duty!"

A man standing at my right grabs my arm. "It's . . . it's
him," he whispers, pale with fright. Craning my neck, I
try to get a better look at the speaker and am in turn struck
with amazement. We know him, he belongs to my work-
team. Except that yesterday, before our return to camp,
he was beaten to death by an overseer. His body was
brought back and left in front of his barracks to be present
at roll call.

"I have come back from there," he says, pointing to
heaven. "And I know the truth. Everything has been taken
from us, everything has been killed in us, even our taste
for joy. If ever, since the beginning of human experience,
there have been men robbed of all earthly attachments, it
is we. Our persecutors have stifled in us even the capacity
to do evil. We observe all the Commandments. We do not
kill, we do not covet, we are neither perjurers nor hypo-
crites. Unlike our executioners, who concentrate on finding
ways to murder man. And so I ask you, brothers: why take
their crimes upon ourselves? Let us have the courage to
proclaim our innocence as well as our determination to sit
in judgment . . ."

Recovered from our first shock, we make him stop. And
the cantor, trembling, starts the *Vidui* again from the
beginning. And the condemned once again recite with him
the traditional deceitful formulas, and try to forget the
interruption.

We say we are guilty, and perhaps that is what we believe. Perhaps we need to consider ourselves guilty because
otherwise it would mean that God does not know what He's

187

doing, and does not do what He wants. Despite the barbed wire or because of it, we try to believe that God exists, and that in His book, everything is indeed inscribed, weighed, set right and fulfilled.

After services I catch another glimpse of the man come back to haunt us. There he is again: moving back and forth through the crowd, he entreats his comrades not to repudiate him, to let their eyes see what he sees and let their faith support his anger. But they refuse to listen.

Someone even says: "You pretend to be dead? The dead no longer impress us."

And another: "You forget where you are. Your truth, you forget that it too is dead."

And a third: "To deny God here, you don't have to be brave; if anything, it's too easy."

Defeated by our unanimous disbelief, our comrade goes back to heaven. There he is advised that he is no longer welcome, having revealed things not meant to be revealed. He is sent back to earth. And if he comes to *Kol Nidre* service, it is to make amends.

. . . The old Jew has come to the end of his tale. I ask: "This angry dead man, who was he? What happened to him afterwards?" And I watch the old man's eyes change color and expression, though they remain glassy. Visibly offended, he cries: "How dare you?"

Then he hurls insults at me and humiliates me because I am "too young to know everything."

Shabbat

The following remark was made by the Israeli writer Moshe Prager:

In the camps, there were *kapos* of German, Polish, Hungarian, Czech, Slovakian, Belgian, Ukrainian, French and Lithuanian extraction. They were Christians, Jews and atheists. Former professors, industrialists, artists, merchants, workers, militants from the right and the left, philosophers and explorers of the soul, Marxists and staunch humanists. And, of course, a few common criminals. But not one *kapo* had been a rabbi.

Prayer

I no longer ask You for either happiness or paradise; all I ask of You is to listen and let me be aware of Your listening.

I no longer ask You to resolve my questions, only to receive them and make them part of You.

I no longer ask You for either rest or wisdom, I only ask You not to close me to gratitude, be it of the most trivial kind, or to surprise and friendship. Love? Love is not Yours to give.

As for my enemies, I do not ask You to punish them or even to enlighten them; I only ask You not to lend them Your mask and Your powers. If You must relinquish one or the other, give them Your powers. But not Your countenance.

They are modest, my requests, and humble. I ask You what I might ask a stranger met by chance at twilight in a barren land.

I ask You, God of Abraham, Isaac and Jacob, to enable me to pronounce these words without betraying the child that transmitted them to me: God of Abraham, Isaac and Jacob, enable me to forgive You and enable the child I once was to forgive me too.

I no longer ask You for the life of that child, nor even for his faith. I only beg You to listen to him and act in such a way that You and I can listen to him together.

Hasidic Celebration

Attended yesterday, Saturday, an unexpected reception in honor of a young professor who comes to this *shtibel* for the same reasons I do: he loves and admires these miraculous survivors of another age who have remained steadfast in their fight against oblivion and sadness.

The officiant had already started the service when one of the worshippers went up to the leader of the small community—Reb Leibele Cywiak—and whispered into his ear: "They say our young visitor is getting married this week."

The service comes to a halt and the Hasidim flock around the bridegroom-to-be to congratulate him and offer their good wishes. Gruffly, Rabbi Cywiak pretends to be offended: "Why didn't you say anything? First of all, tradition requires that you be called to the Torah. Secondly, if I had known, I would have prepared a reception, a true-to-form *Kiddush*. But you wished to deprive us of that pleasure. That is not nice, young man, not nice at all."

"Oh, you know . . . Why trouble you? After all . . ."

"Trouble us, you say? Do you hear him, friends? He deprives us of a good deed and expects us to thank him!

It is now, by taking us unawares, that you trouble us . . .
Not nice, I tell you, not nice at all . . ."

"Forgive me . . . Not important . . . Dislike recep-
tions . . ."

"How selfish can you be? You only think of yourself!
What about us? Don't we count any more? It is written . . ."

"It is written nowhere that the bridegroom must be
entertained before the wedding. During and after—yes.
Not before."

From the privacy of my corner, I observe the young
man. He is moved, but his emotions are under control. He
seems shy, intimidated, that's all. Embarrassed. In the face
of the rabbi's exuberance, he makes an effort not to blush.
He blushes anyway.

I notice the famous thinker A. J. Heschel. He too is
watching the bridegroom.

"Why so melancholy?" I ask him.

"I look at this young man and I see him elsewhere. If
not for the war . . ."

"If not . . ."

". . . I know, I know. But sometimes, in my dreams, I
put out the fire in time. I rediscover myself as I was before. And I remember. The customs of long ago. The
Saturday preceding the wedding the whole town escorted
the young man to the synagogue. He was treated like a
prince and given the place of honor. As he was called to
the Torah, the congregation rose. And after he had recited
the traditional prayers, he was showered with nuts, raisins
and other sweets: symbols of abundance and good wishes.
Then he was escorted home with great pomp. For hours
and hours, there would be singing and dancing and drink-

ing in his honor. The old men told stories, the troubadours composed songs. While now . . ."

"What do you expect?" I say, answering for the young man. "Times have changed, so have customs. We have unlearned the art of inviting joy and fervor."

We both fall silent. We know the young professor lost his parents. It is probably best to leave him to his thoughts.

Meanwhile, it is getting late. The service has been resumed. But Reb Leibele Cywiak and his friends are conferring in a corner:

"What? Let him leave like that, without anything?"

"Empty-handed?"

"Inconceivable . . ."

"Inadmissible . . ."

"Let's arrange . . ."

". . . a reception? In one hour? And on Shabbat, no less? Impossible . . ."

"Even so . . ."

The young visitor is not one of the regulars; but his new status entitles him to full consideration and honors.

All of Israel's children are equal; one must love them equally and, if need be, prove it to them.

"All right," says the rabbi, "don't worry. We'll manage. It will not be said that we are giving up our traditions."

He quickly removes his ritual shawl and disappears behind the door leading to his private quarters. A half hour later he is back, more radiant than ever.

He catches up with the service; in the meantime we have reached the reading of the Torah. A conscientious stage director, the rabbi manages to communicate his secret instructions to the congregants without attracting the groom's attention.

The young man is the last to be called to the bimah. He is reciting the closing benediction when, suddenly, in response to the rabbi's signal, the other men take several steps backwards. Suddenly he finds himself alone. At first he looks lost and frightened. Then his face reflects profound and painful surprise, as nuts and raisins rain down on him, as in years gone by, as though he were still living in a world protected by his father.

I watch him close his eyes and I see the trembling. Through the ripped veil, no doubt, he is seeing the same things my own imagination is retrieving out of the irrevocable past. No doubt he grasps the distance separating him from that past. Any second he will give in: the tears he has held back so long will be allowed to flow.

But no, not here, not now, he seems to be telling himself, I must not let go. Not here, not anywhere, not ever. Think of something else, turn back to the present. You cannot let go. Be careful. Clench your fists until they ache, bite your lips until they bleed: not one tear must be shed. After all, you didn't train your will all these years just to come to this? And with an effort he hopes will go unnoticed, he reads the Haftarah and chants the benedictions; his voice does not betray him a single time.

His duty done, he withdraws into a corner for the second half of the service. More alone than ever, he seems even paler.

But the story does not end here. Reb Leibele Cywiak has further surprises in store: everybody is invited to an improvised reception. No sooner are we seated than we are served wine, liqueurs, vodka and everything else one may expect to find at a Hasidic celebration.

Someone calls out: "Rabbi Cywiak, we didn't know you could work miracles!"

And our host, proud of his exploit, responds: "The continuation of a tradition, that is the true miracle!"

We fill the glasses, we drink to the young man's health and future happiness, we intone one song and then another. Almost like before, almost like over there, on the other side of war. And still the young man remains silent and aloof, breathing deeply, heavily, as if to calm his pounding heart. He gasps for air; his forehead is bathed in perspiration. I know his thoughts are with those who are absent, for his face, his eyes are clouded. If only he knew their resting place, he would follow tradition and go anywhere at all, to invite them to his wedding. But there is no place to go.

At the table, the guests make every effort to cheer him; some try to change his mood by teasing him, others speak to him in whispers.

Reb Leibele Cywiak calls for silence: "One day the Guerer Rebbe, may his sainted memory protect us, decided to question one of his disciples: How is Moshe Yaakov doing?—The disciple didn't know.—What! shouted the Rebbe, you don't know? You pray under the same roof with him, you study the same texts, you serve the same God, you sing the same songs, and you dare tell me you don't know whether Moshe Yaakov is in good health, whether he needs help, advice or comforting?

"Therein lies the very essence of Hasidism," concludes our host, "it requires that every man share in every other man's life and not leave him to himself in either sorrow or joy."

A furtive glance toward the guest of honor; never have I seen him so tense. The basement is only dimly lit but dark glasses shield his eyes. His drawn features betray his turmoil. His lips open and close without a sound. How much longer until his strength gives out?

Other speakers take the floor. In accordance with custom, we now sing the bridegroom's praises. Does he even hear what is being said? The qualities attributed him? The wishes being expressed? His eyes, what do they see at this very moment? What images do they call forth and from what depths? And why does he feel this oppressive desire, this need to weep? And why is he not weeping? Whom is he defying by holding back his tears? His head bowed low, he is sitting among us against his will, dazed and ill at ease, a stranger at his own feast.

Sensing his distress, I want to touch his shoulder and say: Chase away your sadness, lift your eyes and look at the friends surrounding you, don't reject them. But out of discretion, I keep my place and my role.

Professor Heschel, though, takes the initiative by turning toward the guests: "What! Don't you people know how to dance?"

The Hasidim ask for nothing better. Quickly they move tables and benches out of the way. No sooner has a circle been formed than a powerful song rises from the entire congregation: a rapid, torrential song, full of rhythm and fire, a dizzying call to fervor, a song so vital it imposes its mark on the earth. They dance, hand-in-hand, shoulder-to-shoulder, their faces aflame, their hearts filled with joy. The circle gets larger and smaller in turn. The dancers part, come close again, lose and rediscover each other: they become one with the song, they become song. Song has won a victory over silence and solitude: we exist for others as well as for ourselves. And so we sing to cover the noise of all those years reverberating in our memories. And also to show our ancestors: Look, the chain has not been broken. We take up the same song ten times, a hundred times, so as not to leave it, so as not to leave each other. The way it was sung in Wizsnitz and in Sighet. And the Hasidim dance the way they danced in Guer. Louder, faster! May the song become dance, and motion become song. May joy come to orphans and their friends, a joy at once ancestral and personal, violent and serene, a joy that announces and is part of creation.

Since I have remained on the sidelines because of a fractured leg, I am free to watch the participants. From the very beginning of the festivities, the young man has often closed his eyes. Even now he is staring at the floor, his teeth are clenched while he allows the Hasidim to encircle and pull him into their frantic rounds. Does he know what he's doing or where he is? Suddenly I am drawn into the vision: we are in another town, in another synagogue, surrounded by other guests. He recognizes them, he knows them: parents, uncles, cousins, teachers, fellow students, friends. And all murmur: Thank you for inviting us, thank you for allowing us to celebrate this Shabbat with you; we shall come to your wedding.

And that is when, for the first time the defenses fall. Everything is spinning around him, inside him. There is no more reason to feel shame or fear remorse. Through his eyelids, closed as though forever, he feels the flow of his first adult tears: they flow and flow and scorch his face.

And I wonder about his eyes. Whether they are still the same.

JOURNEY'S END

Two legends:

When Rebbe Yishmael's turn came to endure Roman torture, a heavenly voice was heard to say: "Yishmael, my son, keep quiet. If you weep, I shall throw the world back into chaos. One single tear will engulf all of creation."

And Rebbe Yishmael did not weep. In spite of his wounds. In spite of his anger. He destroyed nothing.

Clothed in the mantle of the prophets, young Elisha assembled the villagers and told them a strange and disturbing tale: he had just seen his master flying off—alive in a fiery chariot, straight up to heaven, never to return.

Except for the children, the village did not believe him. So he began again. For the children.

. . . And now, teller of tales, turn the page. Speak to us of other things. Your mad prophets, your old men drunk with nostalgic waiting, your possessed—let them return to their nocturnal enclaves. They have survived their deaths for more than a quarter of a century; that should suffice. If they refuse to go away, at least make them keep quiet. At all costs. By every means. Tell them that silence, more than language, remains the substance and the seal of what was once their universe, and that, like language, it demands to be recognized and transmitted.

About the Author

Elie Wiesel was born in 1928
in the town of Sighet in Transylvania.
He was still a child when he was taken
from his home and sent first to
the Auschwitz concentration camp and
then to Buchenwald. After the holocaust
he was brought to Paris, where he lived
and worked as a journalist and a writer.
He has been an American citizen for some years,
and he and his wife live in New York City
for most of the year, spending the balance
in Paris and Israel.